HISTORIA ECLESIÁSTICA INDIANA

A Franciscan's View
of the Spanish Conquest of Mexico

Fray Gerónimo de Mendieta

Critically reviewed, with selected passages translated
from the original
by
Felix Jay

Studies in the History of Missions
Volume 14

The Edwin Mellen Press
Lewiston/Queenston/Lampeter

Library of Congress Cataloging-in-Publication Data

This book has been registered with the Library of Congress.

This is volume 14 in the continuing series
Studies in History of Missions
Volume 14   ISBN 0-7734-8607-0
SHM Series ISBN 0-88946-068-X

A CIP catalog record for this book is available from the British Library.

Copyright © 1997   The Edwin Mellen Press

The Edwin Mellen Press
Box 450
Lewiston, New York
USA 14092-0450

The Edwin Mellen Press
Box 67
Queenston, Ontario
CANADA L0S 1L0

The Edwin Mellen Press, Ltd.
Lampeter, Dyfed, Wales
UNITED KINGDOM SA48 7DY

Printed in the United States of America

CONTENTS

I

GERÓNIMO DE MENDIETA (c.1524-1604)

The man and his work

The author of the *Historia Eclesiástica Indiana* was born in Vitoria (Alava), but the date of his birth is uncertain. Joaquín García Icazbalceta mentions that Mendieta's father had forty children, of whom Gerónimo was the youngest. At an early age he entered the Order of St Francis in Bilbao, and he arrived in Mexico in June 1554. There he attended the college of Xochimilco, studying Latin, the arts and theology, while at the same time acquiring a remarkable mastery in the lingua franca of New Spain, Náhuatl. A speech impediment prevented him from pronouncing sermons in his own language to his fellow Spaniards, but he developed into an accomplished correspondent and writer, both in his own and in the principal native idiom, and he spent a great deal of his time and life as an archivist as well as editor of his Order's documents. Some of his letters, private and official, have survived.[1]

In many ways his career resembled that of other Franciscans, except that absence from preaching greatly reduced his own missionary effort. He did, however, act as guardian and superior of Franciscan houses, and we find him in places like Tlaxcala, Xochimilco, Tlatelolco, Tepeca and Huexotzinco. His stay in Mexico was interrupted in 1569 when he accompanied Fray Miguel Navarro to the general chapter of his Order, held in Spain, but he returned to the New World in 1573. He died in the monastery of San Francisco el

Grande in Mexico City on 9 May 1604, suffering from a stomach complaint which had plagued him for many years. With his last breath he cited St Augustine: "At this end of my pain, please pardon me for all eternity." He had spent fifty years in New Spain and probably seventy as a friar. They buried him in the monastery, but his ashes were dispersed during the desecrations of the nineteenth century. Most of the biographical details come from Juan de Torquemada (Vol. III, Bk. 20, Ch. 73).

Mendieta wrote one major work, the *Historia eclesiástica indiana*, completed about 1595.[2] In 1596 the manuscript of the *Historia* was sent to Spain for publication. This was the last word heard of it. It meant that the important later historians, for instance Clavijero, Prescott, and Orozco y Berra, were ignorant of it. In 1860 Joaquín García Icazbalceta heard from Madrid that among the papers left by Bartolomé Gallardo they had found the manuscript of the *Historia*. Don García purchased it and in 1870 published it at his own expense. A facsimile of his edition forms the basic text of our study.

The title indicates the nature of the work: the author intends to present the history of the advent of Christianity in the Caribbean and Mexican regions as a consequence of the Spanish Conquest; he intends to illustrate triumph and tragedy connected with the missionary effort and the difficulties in the conversion of the Indians, the conflict between spiritual ends and material interests, all seen through Franciscan eyes. We are therefore essentially dealing with a history of the Franciscan Order in New Spain, and the work may be defined as a specialized record of the most important section of mendicant society which, almost incidentally, cannot avoid filling the wider historical canvas and coming to grips with political, economic and social controversies. Father Juan Domayquia, who wrote a preface, outlined the tenor of the work as follows:

> The specific title *Historia eclesiástica* was chosen because its principal theme and subject matter is the

conversion of souls through the ministry of the servants of the church; the adjective "indian", being a general term, though the book deals solely with New Spain, has been chosen because this was the first territory, following the islands, settled by Spaniards. It saw the beginning of the joyous adventure of discovering a new world and the gateway leading to the conversion of so many infidels who had previously lived in darkness in yonder parts.

The author divides his work into five "Books", each one of which is preceded by a few words indicating their content and main theme:

Book I : "The introduction of the Gospel and the Christian Faith in the Island of Española and neighbouring parts, subsequent upon their discovery." After a brief reference to Columbus and the support he received from the Catholic Monarchs, who made themselves responsible for the new enterprise, backed by an authority from Rome, the evangelizing effort meets with failure in Santo Domingo, where the maltreatment and overwork of the Indians leads to their eventual destruction and extinction. He acquits the Spanish monarchy of any blame for this but points an accusing finger at the Spanish officials and settlers. (17 chapters)

Book II : "The rites and customs of the heathen Indians of New Spain." The book is preceded by a "Prologue for the Christian Reader", citing the main source of his information (see our translation). The book names the principal native deities, rites and festivals, omens and superstitions, education and social discipline, war, criminal law, etc. It introduces Moctezuma. While most of the material concerns the México-Aztecs, some chapters are reserved for other nations. (41 chapters)

Book III : "An account of how the faith of Our Lord Jesus Christ was introduced to the Indians of New Spain."

It starts with the briefest of prologues, reiterating the theme indicated by the heading of the Book. This part of the work introduces Hernando Cortés as a new "Moses" whom Providence has elected for his task. It lists papal bulls authorizing the work of the Franciscan Order in the New World, relates the arrival of the first "Twelve", their reception in Mexico City, etc. It continues with a description of the beginnings of a comprehensive missionary effort, the teaching of native children, difficulties in the introduction of the sacraments, occasional native resistance and the physical destruction of idols. It highlights the linguistic problems as well as the growing mastery of native languages by some of the brethren. (60 chapters)

Book IV : "This book deals with the progress of the christianization of the native."

It begins with another brief prologue pointing out to the "Christian" reader that the previous book concerned itself with the initiation of the missionary effort, while Book IV records the progress made. The author admits that "the fruit of Christianity and its fulfilment and promise have not been as massive as was desirable and had been expected and hoped for"; Christianity itself could not be blamed for this, but "contrarious mundane circumstances".

The initial chapters relate the arrival of Dominican and Augustinian mendicants, the spread of evangelization in Michoacán, Yucatan, Guatemala and Nicaragua. The Book stresses the ability of the natives to learn reading and writing and practical arts, crafts and trades. It comments on the growth of Christian devotion among the newly converted and lists examples of exalted visions and other near-miraculous experiences of native Christians. It condemns the racial prejudices of the Spanish colonists as well as the new social institution of the "Repartimiento" or system of "Encomiendas" (allocation of native labour to Spaniards; this is explained more fully below, see p. .) The Book concludes with miscellanea, such as the presumed traces of earlier Christian influences in the New World, lists of churches and provincials of the Franciscan Order, etc. (46 chapters)

Book V (Part I) : "It relates the lives of the illustrious apostolic missionaries who died a natural death."

This is an unblushing hagiology portraying the lives of the friars who have laboured for the faith in New Spain. There is a prologue, this time a lengthy one, with copious quotations from the Old and the New Testament. Much space (16 chapters) is devoted to the life of Fray Martín de Valencia, the leader of the group of the twelve Franciscans who arrived in Mexico as a vanguard of missionaries. The chapters allotted to Motolinia (Ch. 22), Bishop Zumárraga (Chs. 27-30), and Sahagún (Ch. 41) are of special interest. (58 chapters)

Book V (Part II) : "The Friars Minor who suffered martyrdom while preaching the Holy Gospel in New Spain."

Once more Mendieta treats the reader to a lengthy prologue, starting with a quotation from St John (XV:13): "Greater love hath no man than this, that man lay down his life for his friends." This is followed by quotations taken from Thomas à Kempis, St Chrysostom, Saint Gregory and Saint Bernard. Mendieta devotes the rest of the proem to the Chichimecs, by which he means the barbaric and semi-nomadic dwellers of the vast spaces to the north of Anáhuac and the civilized territories. Taken as a whole, the sequence of names with almost identical careers and disasters, the recital of saintly and meritorious deaths and martyrdoms, becomes boring; but let us be fair, they were not meant for twentieth century readers! (10 chapters)

Mendieta mentions some of his sources: Fray Andrés de Olmos, whose work on Mexican antiquities has unfortunately been lost, another fellow Franciscan, the famous Bernandino de Sahagún, and Toribio de Benavente Motolinia, as well as one Francisco Jiménez, whose work on "The Life of Fray Martín de Valencia" is also lost. He quotes Cortés's *Cartas de Relación* and Bartolomé de Las Casas.

One tantalizing problem however remains: the similarity, and in some cases verbal identity, with Torquemada's text. This has caused Mexicanists a great deal of trouble and still enlivens their debates. The question whether Mendieta copied passages from an earlier manuscript of Torquemada's or vice versa will probably never be solved. It remains an unquestionable fact that certain parts of the two works (Mendieta's *Historia* and Torquemada's *Monarquía Indiana*) are identical. In his introduction to Mendieta's work, Don Joaquín García Icazbalceta attaches a complete list of correspondences (pp. xxxvi-xlv); he found that twelve chapters of Mendieta were practically identical with chapters in Torquemada, that large numbers of other chapters and passages had been circumscribed, and that Book V contained several identical chapters. We know from Torquemada's own hand that he spent many years collecting material and making notes, but his own massive work did not see completion until 1611, while Mendieta put "finis" to his manuscript in 1595. Either Mendieta used material Torquemada had recorded before that date, or Torquemada had access to Mendieta's papers, the latter being more likely because of the dates involved. Yet, seen overall, important differences exist between the two works: Torquemada emerges as a serious thinker, comparer, analyser, and philosopher of history with a vast theological and classical background. Mendieta's vision, noble and pious as it is, remains blinkered by his narrower academic background. It goes beyond the scope of this work to pursue this matter further.

Usually Mendieta's prose is lucid. Only occasionally do his sentences assume undue length; biblical quotations do not swamp the text. He likes to lose himself in minor incidents, odd miracles, visions, the appearance of the devil and demons, disembodied spirits and phantoms, but far be it from us to criticize his innocent faith, for the belief in all this formed part and parcel of the spiritual baggage of the friars. His main purpose in putting his pen to paper was definitely the glorification of the sons of the seraphic father St Francis, almost to the exclusion of the other orders. The contribution of the Dominicans and the Augustinians is acknowledged with obvious reluctance, and only shorter chapters are reserved for them. Only Las Casas, a Dominican, is granted full praise and recognition, but with one reservation: his principal sources of information were those supplied by Franciscans!

Mendieta is probably the most concise exponent of the Franciscan view of the Spanish conquest which assumes divine intervention by heavenly elected leaders, such as Cortés, a "new Moses".[3] The scheme he suggests is therefore of the utmost simplicity: The Creator, represented on earth by the Vicar of Christ in Rome, has charged the Spanish monarchs with the mission of finding the New World and caring for its inhabitants, first and foremost by converting them to the true faith and saving their souls from eternal damnation. Not only did angels impel some unknown pilot to change his course and eventually die in Columbus's house leaving vital navigational information; Fray Pérez de Marchena of La Rábida, an amateur cosmographer, happens to be at hand when Columbus reaches Spain, acting under the guidance of the Holy Spirit. The Spanish Monarchs are not deterred by the dubious reputation of the Genoese adventurer and his seemingly fantastic proposals. Providence chooses Cortés to make up for the loss of faithful in Europe, caused by Martin

Luther's defection, thus adding new Christians in the Indies. Heaven also sends Cortés two interpreters, Doña Marina and Gerónimo Aguilar. The "proofs" of this theory go on and on, and, according to Mendieta, the Holy Spirit inspires all those who go forth to convert and to preach to the natives.

Mendieta's philosophy of history is admirable, but one criticism cannot be avoided: the picture created of the Franciscan missionaries is painted entirely in white; it resembles the ethereal figures in Zurbarán's canvases, lacking the sombre tints of ordinary men; they are "too good to be true". To take one particular case, that of Father Marcos de Niza: Mendieta glosses entirely over the man's dubious reputation, acquired in connection with the expedition to Cíbola and Quivira by Vázquez de Coronado. It had after all been this man's illusions or deliberate fabrications of the wealth of the northern pueblos that persuaded the cautious Viceroy Antonio de Mendoza to embark upon an expensive expedition which in the end became a wild-goose chase (Bk. V (1), Ch. 45). And this brings us, inevitably, back to Mendieta's purpose. While the book relates historical facts, it is not in character a chronicle nor a history. Behind the recital of hardships, martyrdom, undying devotion and the success of the brethren, lacks a purpose, set in motion by a range of serious anxieties. For our friar, whose sincerity is never in doubt, harbours a number of grave concerns, which we may sum up as follows: (a) the missionary zeal, the contempt for the luxuries and pleasure of this world, and the glory of martyrdom have virtually flown; (b) the mass conversion, in terms of pure numbers, has been a success, paganism has been successfully stamped out, and their souls may have been temporarily snatched from the devil's grip; their bodies have responded to the bad example set by the Spanish laity. Since their arrival there has been an increase of crimes related to property, while alcoholism, which had been strictly controlled and severely punished by the pre-Cortesian native rulers, has increased and assumed frightening proportions; games, in particular dice, are on the increase, and not only played by men but also by women; foul language is on the increase, and the respect for one's elders is fading out; (c) the unique privileges and position of the mendicant orders, in particular that of the Friars Minor, have been undermined by the Crown's systematic introduction of a church structure based on parish priests and bishops rather than on brethren of the orders. The many privileges which the early papal bulls conferred on them have become pointless, except perhaps in very distant lands, where occasional zeal and martyrdom can still be found.[4] Mendieta's work now can be seen in a new light: he holds the mirror of a glorious past up for his contemporary brethren while at the same time reminding the secular clergy, who increasingly gain ground, of the glories of the earlier mendicants, to whom they owe everything they have and now enjoy.

Mendieta's dislike of the secular priests is not expressed directly, but makes its indirect appearance in the neglect with which he treats some of its outstanding representatives. To take just one example: The justly famous "Apostle of the Tarascans", Don Vasco de Quiroga, originally a famous judge of the supreme court, ordained priest relatively late in life and, like St Ambrose, raised to an episcopal throne, to be bishop of Michoacán, is dealt with in four short lines (Bk. IV, Ch. 43). This follower of Thomas More created model settlements which attracted world-wide attention, and justly so. By contrast every insignificant brother of his order receives lengthy and honourable mention, and is called "sacro" (holy) or "santo varón" (saintly fellow) and "siervo de Dios" (servant of God).

It remains to examine Mendieta's opinion of the natives to whose conversion and Christian indoctrination he had devoted his life. In the first place he accepted as a fact their innate human quality as opposed to the assumption that they were some sort of a subspecies with less than human characteristics. After all, any doubt in this matter would have meant dissent from the basic royal, papal and Franciscan tenets. To him the natives appeared to lack the gift of creativity; they were, however, capable of learning and imitation. When asked, as some good native Christians did, why they could not be accepted as lay brethren in the Orders, he replied that it was not fear of a relapse into paganism that prevented Indians from entering the Christian priesthood or the Orders. It was, he insisted, their "innate inability to control and command", for they were born to obey. His native charges therefore resembled school children at best, at worst sheep, to be herded and looked after, to be treated with sympathetic and loving firmness, in order that their inborn weakness, defencelessness and deprivation was not exploited by the wolves. Neither Motolinia nor Sahagún ever expressed a similar view to this extreme theory of permanent tutelage of the Indian nations. Nor is it easy to understand how Mendieta could reconcile this view with the historical facts of the Mexican pre-Conquest situation; for not only does he acknowledge Moctezuma's gifts as a ruler of his nation, but he also praises the arts and crafts which the natives practised so successfully in their independent past. That these "obedient sheep" have accepted Christianity so rapidly under the guidance of their shepherds does therefore not surprise him, for he sees it as yet another proof for his theory of their lack of creative genius and talent for submission.

The Franciscans' duty extends to a protection of the natives against the Spanish colonists. The Spaniards, ordained by Providence to conquer the New World and to deprive Satan of hundreds of thousands of souls whom hitherto he held in bondage, blinded by their success and motivated by greed, have abused the Indians entrusted to them; they have overburdened them with work, seized their land and dealt with them as if they were disposable property. Not only the conqueror-colonist but also crown officials, obtaining titles, noble status and wealth, have ignored, Mendieta says, the provisions contained in their grants, and failed to make provision for the welfare of the Indians. He inveighs against corrupt officials. He states that the measures taken by crown officials and their general attitude have been inimical to the work of the mendicant orders. As an instance he cites the first *audiencia* (supreme court) of New Spain, which committed great and grave breaches of the royal policy, while, for a considerable time, the protests of Bishop Zumárraga and of other Franciscans were ignored and the Order and some of its members subjected to persistent persecution (cf. Bk. III, Ch. 50).[5] Among the most detrimental factors to Indian welfare he singles out the system known as the "repartimiento", by which Spaniards receive an allocation of native labour (*encomendados*); in turn they are obliged as *encomenderos* to look after the physical and, in particular, spiritual welfare of their serfs.

Mendieta also reflected on the origin of his natives. He repeated the traditional tale of the emergence of the México-Aztecs from the mythical caves in the land of Atztlán. He also summarized the theories put forward by his contemporaries, with the notable exception of Father José de Acosta, the majority of whom assumed some form of emigration from the ancient Near or Middle East; yet he wisely declined to express an opinion of his own, for the Holy Writ did not specifically mention Indians.

Practically all Mendieta's material, except some personal observations, is secondhand. A comparison with other Franciscan writers, with Motolinia (transparent honesty, unshaken convictions, holy zeal in action), Sahagún (scientific history, ethnography), and Torquemada (encyclopaedic mind) leaves Mendieta in the second rank of Franciscan writers. About one hundred years later, another son of St Francis, Augustín de Vetancurt, in his *Menologio Franciscano* attempted to promote the martyrs of the past to an even higher pinnacle and octave than Mendieta had done. While Mendieta treated many of them like proper saints, Vetancurt's calendar of days of the year reads almost like a book of the lives of canonized saints.

Despite his patent weaknesses and limitations, Mendieta remains a valuable source of information, and for this reason cannot be ignored by the student. This has been generously acknowledged by Mexican historians of the past, in particular by Father Ángel María Garibay, and by Miguel Léon-Portilla in our time.

NOTES

[1] We have had access to four letters: (a) a letter, quoted in full by Juan de Torquemada (Vol. III, Bk. 20, Ch. 73), addressed to Don Francisco Gonzaga, General of the Order, bearing no date; (b) a letter addressed to an unknown, but important personage, dated 20 March 1574 from Mexico City, concerning recruitment for the Order (in *Documentos inéditos*, LIV); (c) a letter addressed to an unkown, dated 8 September 1574, dispatched from Tlatelolco and criticizing the temporal authorities, in *Documentos inéditos*, LV; (d) a letter to King Philip II, dated 15 April 1587, sent from Puebla de Los Angeles; it criticizes the failure of royal officials to render sufficient support to the missionaries; in *Documentos inéditos*, LXVIII. Items (a) and (d) have been partially translated. See translated selections below.

[2] Torquemada (op. cit.): "There is another book in which he collected and summarised the regulations of his province, including letters written on various propositions. I have the manuscript in my possession, and it has helped me greatly in my own work, especially in connexion with the problem of the conversion of the Indians and the lives of the friars . . ."

[3] cf. Book III, Ch. 3, which bears the following heading: "How for the conquest of Mexico, achieved by Don Hernàn Cortes, he appears to have been sent by God like another Moses to liberate the natives from their Egyptian servitude."

[4] J. H. Parry, *The Spanish Seaborne Empire*, p. 168: "The 1570s saw the end of the great age of the missionary activity in New Spain . . . By 1570 the original zealots were all dead, and the excitement and fervour of early days had largely disappeared. The letters of Mendieta, the author of the *Historia Eclesiástica Indiana*, and other leading Franciscans, are full of complaints, not only of persecution by the bishops, but of apathy and chaos within the province. Guardians were resigning and asking to return to Spain; few recruits

were coming forward, and they were ill-trained and ignorant; of the friars who remained few were willing to travel and none would take the trouble to learn native languages . . . The truth was that the mendicant missions in the settled areas had outlived their primitive function . . . the barefoot friar had to give way to the comfortable parish priest, once the spiritual conquest seemed secure."

5 Mendieta's disappointment with the colonial administration and its representatives is passionately expressed in his letter to Philip II (see below).

II

Translated selections from letters written by Mendieta

I Appendix to a letter (undated), addressed to Don Fray Francisco Gonzaga, General of the Order of Friars Minor, in which Mendieta proposes the introduction of confraternities within his Order, the members of which are to pronounce solemn "professions". Another attempt to return members to the strict rule of the order. This letter is to be found on p. 564 of Juan de Torquemada's *Monarquía Indiana*:

Solemnly moved by the desire to assist our Lord God and to serve him freely with Christian and Apostolic zeal, this being essential for my salvation and the general good of religion, I hereby profess and firmly protest the propositions which follow. I shall do my best to observe and guard them and refer to them throughout, with all my power and strength:

<u>Firstly</u> : I promise that in my life I shall not seek office in my own order, nor outside, neither canvass on my own behalf nor in favour of any other person, but to persist with the everpresent hope that God will choose me for such offices where I can best work in His service and for the good of the Christian commonwealth.

<u>Secondly</u> : I pledge myself not to take any temporal advantage, neither for myself nor for anybody else; on the contrary, I shall abhor and avoid, to the best of my ability, any interest in money and treasure which I may find among my brethren.

<u>Thirdly</u> : I promise never to discriminate against the natives of this land or

any others in this my province. I shall be a friend of the virtuous and of the brethren of all other orders who are distinguished by probity and their religious efforts. I shall shun all contacts with heresies and factions, the work of the Devil.

Fourthly : I undertake to commend to God, every day and in particular, those who make or have made a similar pledge, and honour them as true brothers in Christ. I also intend to address to God the following prayer as often as I can:

"All-highest and omnipotent God, our Lord, I, a sinner, unworthy to appear before Your throne, in all humility beseech You to grant us and all others Your grace and compassion, to enable us to enjoy the glorious name of Christians and the devotion to Your honour, glory and sacred service. And for this we shall strive, struggle and work with all our strength, for this is what we treasure and glorify. We abandon all other human urges and desires and any wordly interests, and trust that this will help us to annihilate and totally root out in us all of these aberrations. Please do confound those who harbour vain desires and leave them shattered in order that they may be converted to a desire to seek the eternal God, so incomparable, unique and true! That You may be our God and Lord in this my life. We shall demonstrate to you that as Your servants we shall open the gates through which Your Holy Gospel will be disseminated in all the lands of the infidels and accepted by them with feelings of joy! Ut convertantur ad te omnes gentes, et fiat unum ovile, et unus pastor ecclesiae tuae toto orbe terrarum; et adveniat regnum tuum, et fiat voluntas tua sicut in coelo ita in terra. Amen." (May all gentiles be converted to Your faith, gathered in one fold, with one ecclesiastic shepherd, Your Church for the entire earth. Your kingdom come, Your will be done in Heaven and on earth. Amen.)

II   An excerpt from a letter, addressed to King Philip II
and dated 15 April 1587. In *Documentos inéditos*, No.
LXVIII.

I recall having written a letter to Your Majesty some twenty years ago, which contained twenty-four paragraphs dealing with matters which God had impressed upon me as requiring reform, and which should have received the attention of the governers of these parts.

The first paragraph pronounced a truth and a proposition which I still support as much as I did in my previous letter. It is that Your Majesty has a duty from God to take special care and exercise solicitude for the government of the Indies. And I am quite certain that in the matter of the government of the New World, as well as that of all your other realms Your Majesty exercises as much diligence and care as one could wish. But the duties and concerns connected with so vast an empire spread all over the globe, mean that Your Majesty cannot possibly cope with them except with the assistance of governors, *audiencias* (courts) and councils, in other words, Your Majesty is constrained to govern by means of delegation and through deputies. These men hold offices and act in Your Majesty's name. I shall refrain from commenting on whether they have done their duty or not and whether they have acted in accordance with Your Majesty's principles. But I do know one thing, as an eye-witness in the thirty-three years I have served Your Majesty in this new Church, that ever since the Indians were converted to Christianity the evils and the offences offered to God have reached such a pitch that a personal intervention on your part has become essential and necessary.

I mean by this that Your Majesty will have to lend a hand, in addition to all your other burdens, to further Christian practices among the converted natives, both in their verbal expressions and actions, and, in particular to prevent the Spaniards, who dwell in these parts, from corrupting the natives by the bad example they set. For we shall attract the unfailing wrath of our righteous God, whose punishment, I, a poor sinner, know, will come, seeing that His concerns and service are neglected in favour of mean, selfish and pedestrian interests. I firmly stand by my conviction, my Lord and King and Most Christian Majesty, that if those who governed the land on your behalf, had paid as much attention to the care of souls in the service of God, as to gold and money, God would have, using your Majesty's resources and hand, removed all the heresies which have risen up against the Church. By now the Chinese would have joined the Christian fold in a renovation of the universe. For there can be no doubt that Almighty God, for the sake of the salvation of the world, has placed the burden upon kings of the royal house of Spain, a trust the monarchs should never lose sight of.

It is still not too late for Your Majesty to gain the glorious prize, so far delayed by various obstacles, and this for the sake of the salvation of your own soul, which can be brought about by a renewed effort for the improvement of Christianity in the New World.[1]

NOTES

[1] This letter highlights a typical aspect of the relations of a subject with his king under the Spanish monarchy of that time. Individuals, both lay and clerical, wrote direct to their king. The notion of the autocratic nature of the Habsburg monarchy was certainly correct in some respects, but nothing could have been more "democratic" than a citizen's right to appeal direct to the king. We know that Philip II laboured in the El Escorial, burning the midnight oil, trying to cope with the flood of letters - and of course state documents - which reached him from Spanish, Flemish, Italian and Asian subjects, and even from the Indies. A friar's or churchmen's letter would have had a greater impact than that of a lay person. Men like Motolinia (cf. a famous letter to the King-Emperor Charles V, dated 2 January 1555, attacking Las Casas. Appendix to *Historia*, pp. 203-21) and Bishop Zumárraga, to name two notable Franciscans, regarded the monarch not only their temporal ruler, but also the sacred head of Spanish Christianity.

The letter also highlights the fundamental dilemma of Spanish colonialism created by the Conquest: how to reconcile the political and economic demands of the crown and the *conquistadores* and colonists, with the often utopian and idealistic religious objectives of the mendicant orders.

III

Selections from *Historia Eclesiástica Indiana*

BOOK I

Chapter 1 : Divine Providence at work : The discovery of Española

Christopher Columbus, a Genoese, was the discoverer of the land now called the Indies; he crossed the ocean and found the island of Haiti which he christened Española; he reached it in 1492 with Spanish boats and crews and at the expense of their Catholic Majesties, Ferdinand and Isabel.

The most convincing explanation of this navigational feat lies in the story that many years earlier a Spanish caravel (nobody knows whether it was Basque, Portuguese or of Andalucian origin) sailing in the Atlantic, was driven off course by an easterly wind to an unknown land then not marked on navigational charts. It took the crew a considerable time to find a way back, but eventually they arrived at the island of Madeira where, at that time, Columbus resided. Rumour has it that the caravel carried only the pilot and three or four sailors who, suffering from hunger and their past exertions, died on the island. Columbus, himself a sailor and cartographer, looked after the pilot, whose name remains unknown, but the man died. This left Columbus in possession of all the written material, stored in the caravel, including a description of the long voyage, and this inspired Columbus with the idea of searching for the New World.

Yet Columbus was poor, and an enterprise of such proportions required much money as well as the favours of a king or a great prince, capable of maintaining any discovery. Columbus went from one to the other king, trying first England, then Portugal and later the dukes of Medina Sidonia and Medinaceli, the first-named owning the port of San Lúcar de Barrameda, the latter that of Santa María, both shipbuilding centres; but he had no success. They all took him for a jester or a charlatan, and the plans he submitted for fantastic dreams. Destitute as he was, the only person who gave him credit was a Franciscan friar of the monastery of La Rábida in Andalucia who encouraged him greatly in his project, agreeing with its propositions and exhorting him to persevere. The friar, whose name was Juan Pérez de Marchena, who had already put Columbus in touch with the afore-mentioned dukes, but realising that the two noblemen would not or could not act, advised Columbus to proceed to the court of the Catholic Monarchs with whom he was on good terms. He wrote to Fray Hernando de Talavera, the Queen's confessor.

When Columbus arrived at the court and handed in his petition, the royal couple looked at it, found it most interesting but totally insubstantial. At that moment they were also totally taken up with the war against Granada. Still being monarchs, entirely devoted to the care of souls and the growth of the Holy Catholic faith, they gave Columbus, who in the meantime had secured the backing of Don Pedro Gonzalez de Mendoza, archbishop of Toledo, hope of consideration after the completion of the war against the Moors and the fall of Granada. This then is a summary of the early stages that led to the discovery of lands which now cover enormously large areas and contain in them more faithful souls than the rest of Christian lands.

It remains a marvel how winds could have propelled a boat over more than 1,000 leagues, and we still do not know from which part of Spain that pilot had left; nor whether anybody missed the dead crew nor what name that pilot bore. Is it at all possible that before providing Columbus with ships and crews, our royal couple did not ask him how he had obtained the information on the lands he promised to find for them? Why did they not stop this enterprise at its very root? Did they remain in doubt for a long time after? We can understand all this only by assuming that this was never a purely human enterprise, no fortuitous escapade, but all arranged by Divine Providence; that mysterious pilot and his sailors could well have been impelled and directed by angels, after God had selected Columbus as his instrument, for the setting in motion of the discovery and the paving of the passage to the New World. And He did this to communicate and demonstrate the true faith to a vast multitude of souls, previously in ignorance of the truth. In like manner He selected Hernán Cortés as his agent, and all this for the purpose of the conversion of the untold millions of natives. In the same manner Our God, the ruler of souls, had guided that devout friar, Juan Pérez de Marchena, to insist that Columbus continue his enterprise, humanist and cosmographer as he was. And yet the friar took enormous risks, for though he knew more than Ptolemy, he showed great courage in supporting a theory, suggested to him by a foreign tramp who had wandered from kingdom to kingdom and backing a person everybody else regarded as mad. We are driven to the conclusion that this modest friar and inspired and devout man, was much more than just a cosmopgrapher; he arrived at the certainty of new lands and people, as yet unknown, not by means of his human science but as a result of divine revelation!

Chapter 3 : The monarchs of Castile and their apostolic mission in the Americas

The pre-eminence or prerogative granted to the blessed monarchs of Castile by God Almighty in return for their zeal for the faith, resembles that conceded to the patriarch Abraham, by which he was assured that his lineage would be blessed above all nations. The blessing conferred upon Abraham's descendants was further expanded with the arrival of the Son of God in this world, who was born of the Virgin and descended, in direct line, from the great patriarch. He came to bring about the redemption of the human race, a task in which He succeeded by the sacrifice of His own precious blood. This blessing has now been granted and transferred to the New World and the countless nations discovered therein, and all this is due to the action of the fortunate princes of Spain and their descendants. They sent preachers who introduced the New World to Jesus Christ who had been unknown there. It led to the implanting of the faith in the hearts of innumerable nations, who previously had lived in complete ignorance. These very Indians, speaking of the time when the Gospsel was first preached to them and they accepted it, say: "When Our Lord arrived and came to us", using the expression of a people, fully aware how remote from Him they had previously been. It follows that the title Abraham has among the Hebrews, who call him "Father of the Faith" (and so St Paul called him) could with complete justification be applied by the Indians to our Catholic Monarchs, for it was a result of their zeal and care that the Holy Catholic faith became rooted in Western parts. It follows that we may well call them "parents" of the many nations and the millions of souls, generated by holy baptism.

It is certain that God decreed and commanded these blessed princes to offer Him, the divine majesty, the first-fruits of the conversion, picking, as it were, the first Indians to be baptized from the great multitude. For when Columbus had found the island of Española, he returned to Spain, bringing with him ten Indians and many other objects and products of the New World, all different from their own and much admired by the Spaniards. At that moment the monarchs resided in the city of Barcelona. When Columbus arrived in their presence with only six Indians (the others had died *en route*), Ferdinand and Isabel received the good tidings of the discoveries, and this they did with the utmost pleasure. And when they heard that in those parts men ate one another and that all were idolators, they vowed, with the help of God, to abolish such abominable and inhuman practices and to stamp out idolatry in all lands inhabited by Indians under Spanish control. This represented a vow expressed and fulfilled by them and their successors to the very letter. To prove the seriousness of their holy intentions and to begin the promised work, they ordered the six surviving Indians to be baptized, the two monarchs and Prince Juan, the heir to the throne, acting as godparents.

They sent a dispatch to Rome, giving a report of the newly discovered territories which Columbus had named the "Indies". God had ordained that at that moment the Roman Pontiff was a Spaniard of the House of Borgia, Alexander VI, who with his cardinals, court and the Roman people, was immensely cheered by the news. All were fascinated by the descriptions of those distant parts which until then had been unknown. These newly detected nations were idolators in the clutches and power of Satan; they had to be led to the knowledge of God and on to the path of salvation. In order to bring this about, the Pope, in unison with his cardinals, made a donation to the kings of Castile and Leon of all the islands and mainland discovered or still to be discovered in the Western hemisphere, provided that after a conquest, the kings sent preachers and ministers there to convert and teach the Indians. In confirmation and as authorization of this decision, the Pope sent a bull, in which as supreme pontiff he acknowledged that the Catholic Monarchs, Ferdinand and Isabel had discovered a number of islands in the Atlantic Ocean as well as sighted mainland, all inhabited by a large number of pagans, who hitherto had never been seen or heard of, and that the sovereigns had the intention to submit these territories and their inhabitants for the purpose of converting them to the Holy Catholic faith. In the first place, he praised the holy zeal they had shown and expressed his appreciation of their constant adherence to the Catholic religion; he lauded their efforts to spread the faith for the sake of the salvation of souls, thereby following in the steps of their ancestors, the earlier Spanish rulers. He admonished and requested them, reminding them of the holy baptism they had received through the kindness and compassion of our Lord Jesus Christ, to undertake the task of introducing the pagan nations and residents of the afore-mentioned islands and mainlands to the Christian religion. In order to enable them to discharge this obligation most freely and in a manner chosen by them, though they had never asked for anything themselves, the pontiff with his apostolic authority conferred upon the kings of Spain the gift and sovereignty of all the aforesaid islands and territories of the mainland, discovered or to be discovered; to be defined by a line drawn from north to south from pole to pole, in other words this line was to pass 100 leagues [557.27 km. or 348.29 miles] to the west from the islands known as the Azores and Cape Verde, provided these territories and islands mentioned in the concession, had not been occupied already by another Christian king or prince before Christmas Day 1493. The grant of these lands comprised all kingdoms, towns, castles, places, buildings, fortresses, it conferred rights of ownership and jurisdictions. In return the Holy Father commanded the kings of Spain, in a spirit of holy obedience, which they had already vowed, to dispatch to these islands and mainland territories good, god-fearing, experienced and learned men to teach and instruct the natives in the Christian faith and in civilized behavior. "I command and prohibit all and any person, of whatever rank, status, even of imperial or royal title, not to venture forth to these islands and lands for commercial or any other purpose, without the express permission of the Catholic Monarchs of Spain or their heirs and successors."[1]

Chapter 6 : Father Buil's failure

As we have seen, the Catholic Monarchs had the very best intention regarding the conversion and teaching of the conquered Indians. And had the governors, and other officials, they sent to carry their plans into practice, acted in this spirit and been guided by it, no doubt this world would have given proof of better results than it actually did. All this happened despite the good monarchs giving beneficial orders and making provisions which can only be regarded as adequate. The only neglect of which one may accuse them is that they placed excessive confidence in the persons they sent to the Indies and the advisors accompanying them; the royal pair never suspected that men of known probity and like thinking could be perverted and changed by the lure and attraction of gold and by the contact with a primitive people. During their majesties' stay in Barcelona, when Columbus arrived with the news and his natives, they had decided to provide, as a matter of urgency, ministers for the purpose of introducing the new people to our Catholic religion.

Their majesties chose a monk of the Order of the Blessed St Benedict, a very learned man of impeccable reputation, called Father Buil,[2] a Catalan. Pope Alexander VI invested him with the powers of a vicar-general and head of the Church of those remote lands. With him they sent twelve learned and experienced priests of unblemished character as well as ornaments, crosses, chalices, images and all other items required for divine service and for the decoration of the churches that were to be built. They also made sure that the lay persons who passed to the Indies with the priests were "Old Christians" and of untainted blood. Many noblemen and hidalgos left together with the servants of the Royal Government who were sent to supervise and give support to the holy enterprise of conversion. All this happened on the second voyage, undertaken by Christopher Columbus who bore the title of Admiral of the Indies.[3]

When the party arrived at the island of Española they became aware that the isle had much gold, that its natives were available to provide labour, that it was easy to subdue them, and all these factors combined took precedence over the teaching of the faith of Our Lord Jesus Christ. They brought the Indians under control (there may have been 1½ millions of them) and Columbus distributed them among his soldiers, the colonists and the royal officials. Henceforth they became slaves and serfs. They confined some in the vicinity of mines and forced them to extract the metal from shafts. Those not employed in mines had to contribute quantities of cotton and other commodities. However, this was not the cause of their destruction, for the tribute was still tolerable; but later the unbridled greed took over, and they treated the Indians like slaves for the purpose of collecting gold.

For this Chistopher Columbus cannot be blamed. Some of his companions started this, and thereafter the system was encouraged and legalized by another wicked governor Ovando, as we shall see later on. Father Buil and his companions did baptize a handful of Indians, but very few, and even these, I suspect, did not accept baptism to save their souls but were motivated by the expectancy of material benefits.

Father Buil spent two years on the island, most of the time quarrelling with the Admiral instead of looking after the Indians, protecting their freedom and ensuring better treatment for them. He never punished Spanish soldiers for their ill-treatment of natives or other misdeeds committed. The Benedictine, in his capacity of papal representative, blamed Columbus most severely for everything that went wrong and intervened with him whenever he felt it necessary and commensurate with his office; he even pronounced an interdict, suspending divine offices. As temporal ruler Columbus reacted by ordering that the food rations due to the Father and his priests be stopped. When things had come to this pass, some intervened and effected a reconciliation which, however, lasted a few days only, and the situation became as it had been before. The king then recalled both of them.[4]

Chapter 16 : The destruction of the island Indians

In general we have to confirm that many applied for a royal warrant in order to steal under cover of the royal authority. And in similar fashion many, holding official positions in the Indies, required nothing more than a royal authorization, word, clause or paper, to apply themselves to that purpose, with flying colours satisfying their greed for worldly possessions, and all this without noticing or caring for the damage they caused to other human beings, their own souls and their breach of clearly expressed royal policies. It thus happened that the Christian kings of Spain issued innumerable edicts, *cédulas* and instructions in favour of the Indians, thereby following the dictate of their conscience, formulating the most humane edicts imaginable, but that those who governed the natives in the royal name, neither shared the royal ideals nor followed royal orders, seeking only to impose burdens upon the unfortunate natives, burdens they could not sustain; nor could the natives speak out or offer resistance; and all this they did in their own material interest and that of their friends. The few who endeavoured to comply with the law can be counted on the fingers of my hand.

The royal *cédula* states: "In order to facilitate the conversion of these people and to establish one community of these people and the Christians, we command you to converse with them, deal with them and let them undertake work", which surely means that one should apply all possible reasonable and fair means to ensure that the Indians can work without danger to their lives and health, possessions and families. A work schedule should lay down hours of employment, for they must be given sufficient time to look after their plots and attend to their private affairs. Only men should be employed, no women or children, never the aged, chiefs or princes. Workdays should be interrupted by Sundays and feastdays. Natives should undertake work not as slaves but as freemen, for they are legally free, and it must be understood that they should be courteously invited and hired for definite tasks and for a fixed period like all other freemen, for the royal *cédula* says: "You have to pay each man for the day he has spent working."

Exactly the opposite happened in reality. The governors destroyed the main centres of the population and distributed among the Spaniards all the Indians like beasts or cattle, allotting one hundred to one, fifty to another, to some more, to others less, depending on the workings of the "old-boy-net work". The allocations included children, old people, pregnant women and those who had just given birth, chiefs and even the native rulers of the land. It meant that everybody, old and young, as long as they could stand on their feet, men as well as pregnant women and women with small babies, had to work and slave until they gave up the ghost.

Women had to give up their husbands who were moved to mines, some twenty or more leagues away. The wives remained on Spanish estates, working extremely hard, producing large quantities of the bread eaten there, called *cazabe*,[5] digging the earth to a depth of four palmos and a width of 12 feet. This requires a major effort, even for men, for these people were forced to excavate the soil with wooden spades, lacking iron tools. Apart from this, women were employed in spinning cotton and also more onerous work. It meant that husbands did not see their wives for eight or ten months or even a year. And when eventually they were reunited, they were so emaciated and worn out, as a result of the hard work, that they could no longer cohabitate; they failed to produce offspring. Such children as were born perished because of the hard work, and because starvation prevented mothers from having sufficient milk to feed them. On the island of Cuba, 7,000 children died from hunger in three months. Mothers killed and drowned their children out of despair. When women became pregnant they took herbs to abort the foetus.

The official wage, as laid down by the schedule, amounted to three *blancas*[6] for every two days, something of a joke, because the total remuneration per annum would then amount to one single *castellano*, enough to purchase a comb, a mirror or a string of green or blue stones - a magnificent award! And even then quite often, they received nothing at all. The food they were given was nothing but *cazabe*, of little nutritional value, unless combined with meat of fish; they gave them some chili with it or some other root vegetable resembling our turnip.

Chapter 17 : The destruction of the island Indians (continued), and an apologia for the Spanish Monarchs

The labours imposed on both male and female natives, in the gold mines and in the fields, which, because of their physical debility, were most cruel, became continuous. The Indians had been entrusted and given to the Spaniards as working servants but were kept like slaves or private property, and their masters did with them whatever they wanted. And so, the Spaniard, to whom they had been entrusted, imposed upon them some of the cruellest taskmasters imaginable, called *mineros* in the mines and *estanceros* on estates and cattle ranches, men without soul and pity, who allowed them no rest, beat them with sticks, punched and whipped them, prodded them, called them "dogs" or worse, never relenting and always exerting extreme brutality.

The cruel enormities committed by the taskmasters and the intolerable burden of work imposed upon them, forced some of the Indians to escape to the mountains. In places inhabited by Spaniards, the governor appointed some persons, usually the most respected men in the community, named *visitadores*, who, apart from their normal allocation of Indians and in order to carry out their duties adequately were given another hundred service Indians. These *visitadores* were the best watchdogs or guard-dogs, and their men, the field police, brought before them those they captured in the hills. His trustee or *encomendero* then accused the fugitive Indian, saying he was his, and that "this dog" had refused to serve him. He and others were in the habit of frequently escaping into the hills, they were lazy and rebellious. He wanted them punished. The *visitador* tied the culprit to a post and with his own hands took a tarred whip and gave the Indian many cruel lashes, drawing blood and frequently leaving him dead.

In view of this sort of treatment, the unfortunate Indians, unable to see a remedy for their situation on earth, began to adopt the habit of suicide, either by taking poisonous herbs or by hanging themselves. They did this because they were ignorant of the laws of Christ (and to teach those had been the principal objective of conquering them) and because they had been completely forgotten by the governor. There even was a Spaniard whose workforce of two hundred Indians were about to commit suicide one way or another. He threatened those who survived the mass suicide that if they tried it again, he too would hang himself and follow them down to hell there to torture them even more than before!

Queen Isabel was unable to remedy these abuses, nor did she ever receive notice of their incidence, for a few months after having dispatched her last ordinance, she died. She was succeeded by Don Philip I, her son-in-law, who, so it pleased the Lord, also departed this life after her short reign. And thereafter the kingdom remained without a ruler for two years, leaving the bad Christians of the island with even more freedom and licence to tyrannize the natives.

Our Catholic Monarchs of Spain, in whose reign these things came to pass, must be absolved of all responsibility, for they were ignorant of what went on.[7]

34

BOOK II

Prologue addressed to the Christian reader

It is the purpose of this History to treat chiefly, and in detail, with the conversion of Indians of New Spain and how they were led to the light and clarity of our sacred faith and Christian religion. In order to do this effectively it will be necessary, in the first instance, to take the measure of the errors and blindness of their vain religion, the rites and ceremonies they observed and the kind of society in which they lived. This is precisely what my second book sets out to do. We shall learn from it to what depth human understanding can sink and how the absence of faith and divine grace can cast shadows to darken natural light and lead these unfortunate and infidel Indians into absurd and foolish beliefs. In this we must see a judgement of God, for we Christians are unfortunately not prepared to do for Jesus Christ one hundredth part of what they did for our common enemy, the devil. Christians should be put to shame by the zeal displayed by these heathens of inferior ability and by the fact that in their time of idolatry they observed, as far as moral and social behaviour goes, better customs and rules than they do now as Christians and under our control.

You must know that in 1533 the President of the Royal Audiencia of Mexico [supreme court], Don Sebastián Ramírez de Fuenleal, Bishop of Española, also custodian of the Order of St Francis in New Spain, and the saintly Fray Martín de Valencia, jointly, instructed Father Fray Andrés de Olmos of the same order, then the leading exponent and speaker of the native language of this land and a most reliable and learned man, to produce a book on the antiquities of the Indian natives, with special regard to Mexico, Texcoco and Tlaxcala, in order to preserve the memory of the past and to facilitate the refutation of errors and evils; at the same time he should record whatever good or beneficial aspects he could detect, and all this by making use of everything the natives could remember. And the friar did this, consulting all remaining picture books, still in the possession of chiefs and heads of regions, receiving answers from all the aged he interviewed. He compounded all the information in one bulky tome. Three or four copies were then made and sent to Spain, while the original was entrusted to a friar *en route* for Castile, with the result that not a single copy of the book remained in Mexico. One could, however, remember most of its content for it had been discussed and debated, and the writing itself had taken a considerable time. Later some authorities in Spain maintained that Fray Andrés de Olmos had produced an abridged version of Indian antiquities, while a certain bishop, whom this contention did not satisfy, actually wrote a summary of what he could remember of the content.

I, the author of the present book, was naturally eager to gain knowledge of the antiquities. Many years ago, I contacted Fray Andrés as a principal source from whom much information originated. He told me where I would find a definitive copy, produced in his own hand. And it is from this copy and the writing of Fray Toribio Motolinia, one of the early twelve missionaries, that I have gleaned all that is recorded of the ancient rites of the Indians. And this I have written down, following their examples of brevity and their arrangement of the material, as well as ordering it into chapters.[8]

Chapter 4 : A Mexican creation myth

They credited different gods with the creation of heaven and earth; some ascribed it to Tezcatlipoca, others to Huitzilopochtli and some to Ocelopochtli and still other deities. They took the earth for a goddess and appointed her as a wild frog with a mouth full of blood, saying that she swallowed all she devoured. They had different divinities for different objects and concerns, even one for vice and dirt, called Tlazultéotl; they also imagined that the Sun and the planets were gods.

They figured the creation of the Moon as follows: while the Sun emerged, a fire started in a cave and escaped in the shape of the Moon. In the past there had been five suns, an epoch when food-plants and the fruits of the earth did not flourish and men ate all the wrong things. But the present Sun was good and all upon which it cast its rays prospered.

In their paintings the people of Texcoco give a story of the creation of the first human being, varying from that which a pupil, called Don Lorenzo, told Fray Andrés de Olmos. He stated that his ancestors had originated in the same place as the gods, in other words in the Cave of Cichicomóztoc. And the picture they showed Fray Andrés as evidence depicts the progenitor of those born in the land of Aculma, about two leagues distant from Texcoco and more of less five from the city of Mexico. They say that at nine o'clock in the morning the Sun shot an arrow into the land, creating a cave from which a man emerged, the very first human being, but with a body consisting of nothing more than parts from the armpits upward. Later, from the same cave, arose a woman with a complete body. Asked how the man, lacking most of a human body, could possibly have begotten offspring, they answered with a vile obscenity which we cannot repeat in this book. They said the man's name was Aculmaitl and that the place where it happened took its name from him, *acuma*; *aculli* means "man" and *maitl* "shoulder and arms".[9]

Chapter 7 : The temples of the idols: shape, size and number
The appearance and structure of the temples, built by the Indians for their gods, bear no resemblance to those heard of in Holy Scripture, except perhaps that mentioned in the Book of Joshua which speaks of a huge altar erected by the tribes of Reuben and Gad and half that of Manasseh, during the conquest

of the Holy Land. Once they had settled down, they built, near the River Jordan, an altar of immense size. As this particular edifice is the only one mentioned in the Bible, it will be appropriate to refer to the many large temples, almost endless in number, which existed in this land, and this in order to preserve their memory for posterity; for today all these ancient temples have been obliterated.

In the native language a temple of Satan was called *teocalli*, a word composed of *téotl* (god) and *calli* (house), its meaning therefore being "House of god". In all towns of the Indians, usually in their most prominent location, a large temple enclosure could be found which, from corner to corner, measured the extent of a crossbow shot. In less important places its length measured at least the distance of an arrow-shot, but the enclosure was obviously smaller. It was surrounded by a wall, interrupted by gates leading to the streets and principal highways, all of which focused on the "devil's enclosure". In order to render even greater honour to the temples they laid out their highways with the help of measuring ropes, in absolute straightness for a distance of one or two leagues. From the top of the temple you had a rare view of people crowding the highways and arriving from neighbouring places, heading for the enclosure and a principal temple. Every visitor gave a token of respect and reverence or offered a sacrifice of his own blood, drawn from the ears or some other part of his body.

In the highest and most prominent part of the enclosure rose the pyramidal structure with a square base, its size depending on the importance of the city. In an average town the length of the front base measured about 40 brazas [66.87 m] but more in large cities, less in villages. This pile, irrespective of size, was built in layers or steps, one rising up above the other, but each narrower than the previous one. While the baselength had been 40 brazas, it shrank by now to perhaps only 7 or so. It was along the western facade that the faithful ascended the steps to reach the summit.[10] On the summit you had two large altars, facing east, leaving little additional space for anything else, one altar on the right, the other on the left. Each had its own small precinct with a sanctuary. This applied to the major temples only. The altar sanctuary or chapel in large and often also in medium-sized cities, had three floors, one above the other, rising high and in a round shape. It was in front of these chapels, on the western part, facing the steps, that they left sufficient space for sacrifices. We should add that each of the structures we have mentioned looked like tall towers. The *teocalli* of Mexico City was so high that more than a hundred steps led up to the summit, at least this is what observers said. The temple of Texcoco had five or six steps more than that of Mexico.

The temple enclosures of the principal cities used to contain other sanctuaries or smaller temples of varying size. Some faced east, some west, south or north. No chapel ever contained more than one altar. Each had accommodation for the priests and other servants of the devil-gods. The servants carried water and firewood, for in front of each altar, day and night, braziers were kept alight, and this applied to the rooms also. Temples were whitewashed and kept very clean; some even had small gardens with trees and flowers. Most of the larger temple enclosures harboured another main temple, usually surrounded by its own wall, the upper structure also ending in a kind of spire. These were frequently dedicated to the God of Air, Quetzalcóatl, who had his principal sanctuary in Cholula. He also had many temples in Tlaxcala and Huetzotzinco. A native of Tula, Quetzalcóatl had left his home to live in the provinces of Cholula, Tlaxcala and Huetzothinco.[11] From there he had moved to the coast of Coatzacoaltos and had vanished. They always hoped for his return. When Don Hernán Cortés arrived and they saw his boats, they said the god Quetzalcóatl was arriving, carrying temples upon the waves of the ocean. When the Spaniards disembarked they said they were gods!

The devil was not content with the temples or teocalli we have described, but in every town, every borough, even in every corner he had small patios with one or more prayer places. You also found small sanctuaries on hilltops and other eminences, and along the roads, even small chapels inside maize-fields. All were whitewashed, and when the plaster peeled off, they at once repaired it. The temples of Mexico City and Texcoco rivalled each other in size. The Indians of Cholula fell victims to the madness of the builders of the Tower of Babel by attempting to raise one of their temples to the height of the highest mountain range in the land, though I am sure some of greater altitude exist, as for instance the smoke-emitting volcano not far from Cholula and that of Tlaxcala.[12] In order to achieve this objective, they began to erect a pyramid; but today it has only modest measurements, for the greater part of it has crumbled or been demolished; originally it has been much wider, longer and higher. The ancients relate that as they proceeded with their work, God confounded them, not by confusing their tongues but with a terrible storm, thunder and lightning, with large blocks of stone coming down like hailstones, some in the shape of toads, events which naturally frightened them. They took this for a bad omen, stopped work and left the effort once and for all.[13] You find also many temples, complete with platforms, near the village of Teotihuacán, and I can affirm that one in particular (Pyramid of the Sun) is of an enormous size with its summit still crowned with a stone idol. I have seen it myself, for it has so far not been removed, as no means exists of lowering it and disposing of it.

Chapter 12 : Phantoms and the Devil

In their heathen past the Indians worshipped a god who in reality was a phantom or frightening spirit, for it scared people at times. They called it *Tlacateólotl* or "Owl" and thought of it as a person giving the impression of an owl; the word is composed of *tlácatl* = person, and *teólotl* = owl, for an owl looks repulsive and its sad song terrified them at night. Even in our days they are terrified and many regard it as a bad omen.

Even after their having become Christians the phantom appeared to some Indians in that shape. I and other friars learnt this from the natives who, exceedingly scared, came to us after having seen the apparition. For Satan chooses the timid and those of faint hearts, bent on troubling them in order to undermine their faith.

At one stage a chief of Amequemaca told a friar that the devil had appeared to his father in the shape of a female monkey, which jumped from one of his shoulders to the other. At other times the phantom materializes in the shape of a very tall person. One man, particularly brave and intrepid, would not let the phantom go until it made promises to him and showed him special favours, such as helping him in capturing a prisoner-of-war; this would have increased his prestige and given him promotion.

When the saintly Father Andrés de Olmos, so they report, stayed in the monastery of Cuernavaca, Satan appeared to an Indian in the shape of a chief or cacique, richly attired and covered in gold and jewels; this happened in a field and in the morning, Satan said: "Go and tell your chief that because he has forgotten and ignored me for a long time, I command that his people arrange a fête in my honour and at the foot of the mountain, for I cannot make my entry into your town where a cross is barring me access." Saying this Satan vanished. They did what the devil had bidden them to do, and the cacique, whose name was Don Juan, called the people together. They staged the celebrations and offered sacrifices. One of the friars' pupils discovered what had occured, and the people who had staged the festivity were imprisoned and heavily punished. But Father Andrés took pity on the newly converted and asked the Indian to whom Satan had appeared, how this had come about. He heard that the cause had been lack of faith as well as secretly continued worship of the ancient idols. Satan had chosen this man as his messenger for the purpose of leading all others astray. Father Andrés actually wrote down the incantation they had used in which they had implored their god to be released from this life, for they were held in bondage by strangers who had taken all their land.[14]

Chapter 13 : The giants of New Spain

At the time of the conquest of New Spain by the Spaniards, ancient Indians remembered that their land, in past ages, harboured giants. This is a definite fact, for on various occasions and in diverse places, bones of excessively large human beings have been found. Father Andrés de Olmos, dealing with this matter, says that in the days of the Viceroy Antonio de Mendoza [1535-51], he himself has seen in the viceregal palace in Mexico the foot-bones of a giant, with toes about 21 cm long. I personally remember that they presented the Viceroy Don Luis Velasco (1590-95) with the bones and teeth of some terrible giants. We also have examples of men of abnormal, almost gigantic, size in our own time, for instance in the town of Cuernavaca, a man 2¾ varas [c. 2.3 m] in height. They brought him to Mexico City on several occasions where he took part in the Corpus Christi procession. There they gave him plenty of food, but he died in Cuernavaca from starvation. We knew another fellow in Tecalli, who, I believe, was even taller, though exceedingly thin in contrast with the previously mentioned man who was robust and well shaped. They also brought this man from Tecalli to Mexico, to display him as a rare and curious phenomenon, but shortly after returning to his native place he died.[15]

Native belief in the existence of the soul

The Indians held various opinions of the soul. The Otomí,[16] who have a language of their own, thought, being somewhat backward, that the soul died when the physical body expired. Yet in general the people of New Spain and in particular those who shared a common language, the Nahua, held that the expiring body releases the soul, which then went to different locations. They distinguished between various regions, depending on the social status of the departed and the manner of his death. They said that those who died from lightning went to a place called Tlacocán, the residence of the Tlaloques or water-gods. Those who died in battle went to the House of the Sun. Those who died from an illness, they said, had to remain on earth for a while; and because of this relatives provided them with clothing and other necessities which you find in graves. After a certain time the dead went to hell, reaching it after passing nine stations. In the end they had to pass a broad river and there they remained for ever in the company of a reddish dog. This resembles the myth of the River Styx and the dog Cerberus, cultivated by our Old World pagans.

The men of Tlaxcala believed that the souls of their princes and nobles turned into some sort of a haze or cloud or even into birds of rich plumage or precious stones of great value. Meanwhile the souls of commoners turned into weasels, malodourous dung-beetles, or animals producing stinking urine, beasts of rat-like appearance.

You find among them many other versions, as you have to expect from people lacking the illumination of the true faith.[17]

Chapter 29 : Native penal law and prisons

They sentenced to death all who committed grave crimes such as homicide;

he who killed another had to die for it. When a woman terminated a pregnancy with means supplied by, or aided by, another, both women had to die. Women were always attended by female healers, and men by male ones.

He who raped a virgin, either in her father's house or elsewhere, had to die for the offence. He who gave poison to another person, causing his or her death, and also he who prepared it, died. If a husband killed his wife because she had committed adultery, even if he had surprised her in the act, he was sentenced to death for having taken the law into his own hands; he should have gone to court to have her punished. A woman who committed adultery, as well as her male partner, if seriously suspected or caught in the act, were arrested, and if they refused to confess, submitted to torture; after having confessed they were sentenced to die. Sometimes the sentence was executed by tying up their hands and feet and spreading the couple out on the ground; a heavy stone then crushed their heads with an impact so powerful that after a few minutes their heads looked like pulp. Others were garrotted or burnt. Chiefs, after having been hanged, had their heads decorated with feathers mixed with green tufts. The judges ordered adulterers to be taken to the plaza in front of a large public and with their hands manacled; yet those who were stoned there, did not have to suffer very long, and death arrived quickly.

Those who committed adultery while drunk were not spared on account of their intoxication but punished like all the others. A man who slept with his stepmother suffered a similar fate, and she too if she had consented; the same applied to incest between brother and sister, irrespective of whether they were children of the same parents or shared only one father or one mother; this was also the punishment for intercourse with a stepdaughter. Therefore all who committed incest received a death sentence, except brothers and sisters-in-law, for when a brother died, another brother was expected to marry the widow or widows of the dead brother and also adopt her children, a measure resembling the provisions of the Mosaic Law and the principle of *quasi ad suscitandum semen fratris.*

The punishment of bawds, after the discovery of their disreputable trade, was public exposure in the plaza; there they set their hair on fire with the help of a torch until the flame scorched their skull, and in this condition they were released, ever after carrying a stigma of shame. However, if the procurer or procurers had noble status, they suffered the supreme penalty. Nezahualpilli, King of Texcoco, dealt with a bawd who had smuggled a young gentleman who had fallen in love with the king's daughter, into the palace. He was discovered and both were hanged.

Both the active and the passive participant in a homosexual act had to die. From time to time the authorities made a search for sodomists in order to round them up and eliminate them; for they knew very well that this horrible vice was unnatural and therefore did not occur among animals.[18] Bestiality did not occur among the natives. A man who adopted feminine clothing and a woman who dressed like a man were also condemned to die. [There follows information on punishment for offences against property, which in all major details agree with Nezahualcóyotl's legal provisions in Texcoco.] Conspirators or those who committed high treason and attempted to overthrow the head of state or even remove the lowest chief or person in authority, suffered the death penalty.

The condition of the prisons was inhuman, especially for those who awaited execution, and for prisoners-of-war, destined to be sacrificed. The prisons were dank and almost without light, and the cells resembled cages. Access was by means of an opening as small as that of a pigeon-loft, and this "door" was barricaded on the outside with planks held in position by large stones and guarded by warders. The inhuman condition of the gaols induced a rapid deterioration of their unfortunate inmates. They weakened, looked pale and this as a result also of the food they were given, which was both deficient in quality and quantity. They presented a pitiful sight, and most likely they preferred death to suffering in captivity. Prisons usually adjoined the courts, much the same as ours, and they were reserved for serious criminals, awaiting execution.

Less serious offenders were caged in pens, surrounded by a fence of wooden stakes. It occurs to me that in their case all that was required was the drawing of a line on the ground, indicating to them not to pass beyond the line. They would simply not have dared to contravene such an order, for they would never have got very far. With my own eyes I have seen such enclosures, all of them completely unguarded.[19]

Chapter 30 : Drinking and drunkenness : before and after the Conquest

After the conquest of New Spain, the Indians everywhere, men and women, but in particular the common people, began to drink heavily and get drunk. It appears that the devil, deeply upset at losing control of these people as a result of the preaching of the Gospel, managed to coerce them into this vice in order to prevent them from being proper Christians. The circumstances and changes accompanying the Spanish seizure of the country made this relatively easy for it left the native rulers and Indian judges in a state of impotence and without the authority with which they had previously carried out their functions. This led to general licence in which a person was permitted to drink until he dropped and lost his senses.

This had not been so in pagan times. Drunkenness had been condemned as a great evil in the same way as it is regarded by us Spaniards as something vile. Native societies punished inebriety with the utmost rigour of the law. The consumption of alcoholic drink was strictly regulated by the kings and the judges, and not generally permitted, except in the case of older men and women of more than fifty years of age; it was held that drink refreshed old people's blood and helped them to keep warm and sleep. They drank two or three small cups, at the most four, which did not intoxicate them, for their wine,[20] to inebriate, has to be drunk in larger quantities. Castilian wine is much stronger than pulque and more intoxicating. Native men and women soon became aware of this. In the olden days at weddings, feastdays, and special functions, the natives had been permitted to drink. Medical practitioners used to dispense their medicaments in conjunction with a cup of pulque. During their delivery, women in childbirth were usually given a little pulque, not as a treat, but as a necessary stimulant. Common labourers transporting timber from the mountains or carving heavy blocks of stone were also licensed to drink a few more cups to receive added physical strength and encouragement in their hard work. Kings and princes never took pulque. Their favourite drink was cacao, which is a fruit dried in the manner of almonds; it also serves as currency. The nuts are mixed with water and other beverages made of seeds. Although the natives had a weakness for alcohol, they never lost restraint as they do today; they observed moderation perhaps less for reasons of virtue than fear of punishment.

The punishment meted out to drunken men and even to those who were just feeling the onset of inebriety, singing or talking loudly, consisted of the cutting off of their hair in the most shameful manner in the public plaza. Thereafter they demolished the culprit's house, implying that a drunkard had no right to have a home in a town, that he had not the makings of a proper neighbour but was like a wild beast, having lost his reason and proper judgement. Henceforth he was to live in the open country like an animal. Those convicted of drunkenness were debarred from holding public office.

Today the governors, sheriffs, constables, and magistrates, all have an opportunity to get drunk every day. There is nobody and nothing to stop them, except those who supply alcoholic drink! May God remedy this, for it causes damage to men's souls, and the natives alone are powerless to change this situation.[21]

Chapter 32 : The origin of the Mexicans

Let us now turn to the question how these people reached Mexico. We do not know when they arrived. Some say it happened more or less 600 years ago, but given the unreliability of their chronology, it remains impossible to verify this. Fray Andrés de Olmos offered the following alternatives: either they came from the land of Babel after the division of languages and the destruction of the city the sons of Noah had built, or at the time when the children of Israel entered the promised land and dispersed the Canaanites, Amorites and Jesubites.

Others maintain that these people took their origin from the captive and dispersed tribes of the Kingdom of Israel or even that they were the descendants of refugees from the last destruction of the Temple of Jerusalem by Titus and Vespasian, the Roman emperors. Yet because none of these opinions make sense and have any foundation which could serve as a basis for a judgement or a reasonable argument, it will be best to leave the problem alone and allow everyone to think what he fancies best.[22]

Chapter 36 : Moctezuma : Last king of the Mexican nation

In 1502, Moctezuma, the second of his name, son of Axayácatl, succeeded to the throne of Mexico. The empire of the Aztecs was then at its height and he, endowed with a grave sense of purpose, increased the frontiers of his realm further. In this he was greatly assisted by Tlacaélel, one of his most valorous captains.[23] His outstanding qualities enabled him to seize almost the entire territory of New Spain, and as emperor he kept many kings and great princes as vassals and tributaries. As a prudent and astute man, trained also in the arts of astrology and magic within the limits of the knowledge then prevailing, he was much feared by his subjects, so much so that when they addressed him, they dared not look him in the face but bowed their heads, staring at the ground. This is how much his imposing majesty meant to them. He had a cruel streak but was, nevertheless, a good statesman and administrator. He not only respected and maintained the law and ordinances of his ancestors, but added his own if he felt they needed amending. He imposed heavy penalties and was relentless in his punishment.

He laid down the principles of his judicial system by appointing ordinary judges, like our *alcaldes*, and instituted appeal courts; appeals would reach his own council. This was composed of higher judges, men of governmental, legal and administrative experience, wise and prudent, who were assigned a separate hall in his palace. Another hall housed his council of war which dealt with matters of a military nature and consisted of the generals who had commanded his victorious armies. The king dealt himself with individual judicial cases, and none ever suffered any delay.

His Majesty owned many large houses, full of women, all the daughters of princes. He took those of the highest rank as his legitimate wives in accordance with strict customs, and he derived a large offspring from them. The legitimate wives were the most respected.

In each city of his subject provinces he placed governors and *calpixques* [overseers, administrators, caretakers] who served as sheriffs and local judges and kept overall control. All such officials belonged to the Aztec nobility and were usually appointed according to their merit. They were expected to keep law and order in the provinces, to collect the tribute and to prevent rebellion. In his reign his nation captured 44 towns.

In the sixteenth year of his reign he received news that certain Spaniards had reached the coast, that Cortés had landed, and what they did. In the seventeenth year of his reign, the Marqués del Valle [Cortés] arrived with his men in the city of Mexico. In the following year, the eighteenth of his reign, he died, aged fifty-three, for on his accession he had been thirty-five.

A year later Hernán Cortés conquered the city of Mexico. Because Moctezuma's splendour and his majestic lifestyle have been much described by other authors, on some of whom I have relied, this will have to suffice.[24]

Chapter 40 : Royal funerals

On the death of a king they notified all the neighbouring cities and kings and all other rulers related to or on terms of friendship with the deceased monarch. At the same time they gave the date of the funeral, usually held within four days to avoid the foul smell emanating from the decomposing corpse. Meanwhile they kept the body in the dead monarch's palace and laid it out on a mat, wrapped in a shroud.

The kings and other principal rulers arrived at the funeral, and to honour the departed they brought feathers, cloaks and shields, ornamented with plumage, and small flags, as well as slaves to be sacrificed in his honour. When all were assembled, they prepared the corpse, wrapping it into fifteen or twenty richly worked blankets; they placed in his mouth an emerald, signifying the heart. They also decorated the breasts of the idols with fine gems, representing the heart, a gesture meaning that the stones would confer upon the body and the images true life. Before wrapping the body, they cut off a lock of hair from the top of the head, which, they said, preserved the memory of his soul, his beginning and his end. They preserved this hair together with the lock cut off at his birth and placed it into a box, the inside of which was painted with pictures of the gods. Once the face of the dead monarch had been protected with a cloth, they covered it with a painted mask, while, at the same time, killing a slave. They decorated the corpse further with emblems of their principal deity in whose patio the ashes were eventually laid to rest. All the wives, relatives, friends and fellow princes broke into tears when the time of the disposal of the body arrived. Others chanted, but their singing was not accompanied by the sound of drums, nor did anyone sing when the drums were beaten.

When the cortège arrived at the gate leading into the temple enclosure, the high priest and his ministers came out to receive the corpse; they deposited the body at the base and in front of the temple. And there, decorated as it was with much gold, silver, and precious stones, they set it on fire with the help of a torch and together with their incense, copal or curbaril.[25] The slave they had sacrificed earlier on in the palace had been the servant who performed the duty of lighting and maintaining the fires of the domestic altars and sanctuaries; they had killed him so that he could perform similar duties for his dead king in the life beyond. While the corpse was incinerated, they simultaneously sacrificed a hundred or two hundred slaves, the number of victims depending on the rank and importance of the deceased. They sacrificed them by opening their chests with a flint knife and taking out the pulsating heart and offering it to Satan; subsequently they cast the bodies of the slain down to where the dead king's body was consumed by flames. Some of these slaves had been brought by the king's relatives and friends as a personal contribution, others had formed part of the domestic establishment, men and women, dwarfs, hunchbacks and deformed people who served and entertained royalty. They all had to die to render service in the afterlife, in the same manner in which they had served hereunder. They even dressed them in new clothes, some of which were thinner, to prevent overheating by the Sun. Some sources state that before the incineration they placed in front of the corpse plenty of food as well as maize, as a symbol of the supplies he needed in the nether world, but the Indians deny this. It can, however, be confirmed that during these rites they used to lament and weep and pronounce words like "Let us sing and be merry for once we die we shall shed tears in hell."

In order to guide and lead the departed on his way, they killed a dog by driving an arrow through its neck. They placed the dead dog in front of the corpse, saying that the animal would guide him safely along the tortuous and bad paths and on the passage through canyons and deserts. They were convinced that without the assistance of the dog the passage would become impossible.[26]

The day after, they collected the dead king's ashes and any particles of bones. They placed the relics, together with the lock of hair, into the box and locked it after having put the emerald there too. On top of this box they shaped a wooden likeness of the deceased, and once this was placed in position, the relatives and wives of the dead man began their intercessional prayers which they called *Quitonaltiaya*. This took four days, and was accompanied by offerings in front of the image and the box; it had to be performed twice daily. On the fourth day the principal honours had been completed and this was accompanied by the slaughter of another ten or fifteen slaves. They said that during these four days the soul had started its pilgrimage and that their prayers supported it.

Twenty days later they sacrificed another four or five slaves, forty days later another two or three, sixty days on, one or two, and after eighty days ten, the exact number to be slain depending on the status and importance of the deceased. This marked the end of the killing of slaves. Yet they held a memorial service in front of the image and the box annually, sacrificing quails, rabbits, birds, butterflies, pulque, maize, seashells and small étuis containing perfume. This went on for another four years. Meanwhile the survivors honoured the dead man's memory with dances by getting drunk and shedding tears, and they took the opportunity of combining this with mourning also other deceased persons.[27]

BOOK III

Chapter 1 : Hernando Cortés : a new Moses

In the year of the Lord 1519, when Pope Leo X reigned in Rome as supreme Pontiff and when the most Catholic Emperor Charles, fifth of that name, was the most blessed king of all the Spains, head of all Christian princes, the most illustrious and enterprising Captain Don Hernando Cortés, later rewarded with the title of Marqués del Valle, landed with 400 Spaniards in a port of the mainland, since called Anáhuac. This name means "vicinity of waters" or "beside the water", because the country is located between two oceans, the Pacific and the Atlantic. Today we know it under the name of "New Spain". Cortés arrived to conquer and acquire it.[28]

Cortés scuttled the boats in which he had arrived in order to deprive his companions of the hope and opportunity of quitting. He invaded the interior and gradually subdued it, partly by means of clever diplomacy and persuasion and peaceful means, making friends with the assistance of his interpreter Marina or Malinche with whom God had supplied him. After his arrival at the coast of Yucatan, he advanced, sometimes fighting, and gained the friendship of the Republic of Tlaxcala, the arch-enemy and rival of the Mexican empire. With God's help and the assistance of other Indian allies, after much fighting and toil he finally gained victory and took the great city of Mexico, capital of the Aztec empire, in the year 1521, on the day of the holy martyrs Hyppolytus and Cassianus, on the 13th August, as is recorded.[29]

The land of Anáhuac comprised the empire of Moctezuma of Mexico and his allied kings and princes, 400 leagues [2,229.08 km. or 1,393.18 miles] in length and 150 leagues [835,905 km. or 522,44 miles] in width, measured from Acapulco to the port of Tampico, from the Pacific to the Atlantic. Some parts are narrower than others. The land of Anáhuac acquired its name of

New Spain as a result of the clemency of its climate and its fertility. At the time of the conquest it was divided into provinces of many different languages and customs, inhabited by a large number of Indians. It was a marvel to see masses of people moving along busy roads like armies of ants. The size of the population was such as to strike terror into the hearts of the few Spaniards who accompanied Cortés.

This simply must lead us to the conviction and conclusion that God, without doubt, had specifically elected Cortés and had appointed this courageous Captain Don Hernando Cortés as his instrument to open the door and the path for the preachers of the Gospel in the New World, as well as to compensate the Holy Catholic Church with the conversion of so many souls for the great losses caused and damage done by that accursed Luther to ancient Christianity at about the same time. It follows that while one part was lost, another was gained. It is surely a miracle that in the same year as Luther was born in Eisleben, a town in Saxony, Hernán Cortés was born in Medellín, a city of Spain.[30] Luther was born to disturb the world and to place under the banner of Satan many of the faithful, whose fathers and grandfathers had been Catholics for ever so many years. By contrast, Cortés sowed the seed of a church of an infinite multitude of nations who for centuries had been in the power of Satan, enmeshed in vice and blinded by idolatry. In the very year of 1519 Luther began to corrupt the Gospel among Christians, while Cortés spread it in his loyal and sincere manner among nations who had never before been aware of it or heard the message of Christ.

This finds its confirmation also in another event in Indian history. In the year of Cortés's birth, 1485, they celebrated most solemnly, in the city of Mexico, the dedication of their principal temple and its idols. On this occasion they sacrificed 80,400 human beings. You can see that the clamour of so many souls and that so much blood spilled, an offence against the Creator, was sufficient cause for God to say: "I have surely seen the affliction of my people" (Exodus III). God wished to send somebody in His name to remedy such great evil, appointing one like Moses in Egypt. Cortés was born in the very year and even on the first day of that great massacre [??], and this is a definite sign and evidence of Cortés's election! With the respect to our comparison with Moses, it does appear that God (and we may call this a miracle) has provided Cortés, who was like a dumb man among the Indians, unable to talk business in their idiom, with adequate interpreters. Moses stammered, and did not God give him the gift to speak Pharaoh's language in front of him? God also allowed him to be understood by his own people. Cortés's interpreters were firstly the Indian, Marina, a native of Mexico, whom he found on the coast of Yucatan, and who had been a captive in Potinchán; she knew the Maya language and had not forgotten her own [i.e. Náhuatl]. The second interpreter was Gerónimo de Aguilar, a Spaniard who had been a prisoner for eight years. Finding him must be regarded as a true miracle and the work of Divine Providence. It was at Cozumel that Cortés heard of him. So he sent a boat with some Spaniards and two Indians to the shores of Pochotán. The Indians had offered to look inland for this Aguilar, in spite of his being in the hands of the enemy; they had been asked to give him a letter with which they had been entrusted. The Spanish crew gave the Indians two days to return, but when they failed to come back within a whole week, the Spaniards returned with their boat to Cozumel, reporting that the Indians had most likely been captured or killed by the men of Pochotán. Disappointed, Cortés sailed. All his ships had been overhauled, but it pleased God to cause a leak in Alvarado's vessel, and this meant a return to Cozumel for repairs. It was at that moment that the two Indians returned in a canoe, bringing with them Gerónimo de Aguilar. Canoes were the traditional vessels of those natives.

The divine election of Cortés to become the leader of a spiritual crusade, is in no lesser manner confirmed by the extraordinary determination which God planted into his heart, when, with little more that 400 Christians, in a land inhabited by innumerable heathens, engaged among themselves in continuous warfare, and with Cortés wholly and totally remote from any human help, he succeeded, even in the face of a complete absence of any possible retreat across the sea. By all standards all this challenges human reason by its very temerity. It contradicted Cortés's habitual prudence; he simply could not have done what he did, unless God implanted in him the conviction that his undertaking was secure and its outcome a certainty. Did not Moses fearlessly go to see Pharaoh? With a boldness looking like the utmost madness, he made friends with those of Cempoala, Huexotzinco and Tlaxcala, without the help of whom it would normally have been impossible to maintain himself and his men, let alone to conquer Mexico and other provinces. Can we possibly credit with responsibility for all this, anything but Divine Providence? This it was that delivered him and preserved him in the face of enormous dangers and helped him in the difficulties he encountered. History relates them, and they are too numerous to be told once more by us.

To comprehend even more clearly God's mysterious choice of Cortés, singling him out for this enterprise, it will suffice to stress the great zeal Cortés displayed for the honour and in the service of God and his efforts for the salvation of souls. These aspects demonstrate the principal purpose of the entire enterprise. For this Cortés set out from Cuba and as proof of his mission he had on all the banners of his ships, in the centre of his coat of arms, placed a red cross with the following inscription: "*Amici, sequamur crucem; si enim fidem habuerimus, in hoc signi vinceremus!*" ["Friends, we follow the Cross! If we honestly believe in it, we shall be victorious"]. He did not enter a single Indian territory where he did not destroy the idols and prohibit human sacrifices. He erected crosses everywhere and had sermons spread the knowledge of the true God and his only begotten son Our Lord Jesus Christ. Not all victorious captains, nor even the princes, always took this seriously. Consideration must also be given to his care and concern for the installation of ministers to effect the conversion of the native people; also to the acknowledgement, authority, and love the Indians themselves extended to him when they received God's gifts with the greatest reverence, a subject we shall discuss later. It is within the spirit and intention of this book to stress this aspect.

I am fully aware of the fact that some writers, among them even very serious authors, have in their works condemned Cortés and have, because of some particular excesses, openly called him a tyrant. I, however, cannot but find excuses for him. Let us consider the facts: what do you expect a man to do who is surrounded by such a multitude of enemies, some open, others hidden (for who can possibly trust a disloyal friend?) who with such few companions has yet to care for them, knowing full well that all are greedy for gold and willing to forsake him and their comrades? How could he prevent at times some of his men robbing, using force or clubbing to death one who stood in their way? He might sometimes have pronounced an unjust sentence of death, saying: "hang that Indian, burn another, apply torture to so-and-so!" He had to give such orders in the case of people of small account, men who killed Spaniards, men who conspired, mutinied or plotted a rebellion, all malefactors. Even in instances in which he was not entirely convinced of the justification of a sentence, he had to give way to the views of his army and his supporters, for he did not wish them to become his enemies nor to be abandoned by them.

Cortés himself, at the end of his Third Carta which he wrote to the Emperor Charles V, after the conquest of Mexico, had to admit that the Indian natives of New Spain had enough understanding and reason to be

58

regarded as average specimens of the human race. Therefore it would be a great wrong if they were treated as slaves by the Spaniards, as had been the fate of the Caribbean Indians. Under pressure, however, of his Spaniards, he states that he could not exempt them from providing labour and that he had been compelled to force the chiefs and the commoners of those parts to maintain and serve the Spaniards, pending instructions from higher authority. In this most important and serious matter he thereby confessed that he had to act contrary to his better convictions. Can we then hold him responsible for matters of considerably less importance?[31]

Chapter 5 :   Pope Leo X's bull in favour of two Franciscan friars [25/IV/1521]

In this bull the supreme Pontiff granted two Franciscans, Francisco de los Ángeles and Juan Clapión, the privilege in the "Indies of the Ocean Seas" freely and without hindrance to preach, baptize, confess, lift excommunication, solemnize marriages, deal with matrimonial causes and to administer the sacraments of the Eucharist and Extreme Unction, and all this without the participation of the secular clergy, ministers, bishops and patriarchs. If another person, irrespective of his clerical status, interfered with them or obstructed them, they would be excommunicated and condemned to eternal damnation. This spiritual punishment could not be mitigated except by the supreme pontiff himself or the superior of the order. The Pope also conferred upon the Franciscan friars the power, in the absence of a bishop, to consecrate altars and chalices, to bless new churches, to appoint ministers and to grant any of the privileges and indulgences normally the prerogative of bishops. They were also empowered to confirm the faithful, as well as to confer the first tonsure upon novices in the Franciscan Order. They were to undertake all the aforesaid duties in order to glorify the name of the Lord, achieve the conversion of infidels, to increase the Holy Catholic Faith and to rebut and destroy anything they found contrary to the ordinances and resolutions of the Holy See.[32]

Chapter 6 :   Pope Hadrian VI confers plenary power upon friars of the mendicant orders ("Exponi nobis fecisti" - 9 May 1522)

In this bull the supreme Pontiff lays down that all friars, belonging to the mendicant orders, especially the *frailes menores* [Franciscans] of the strict observance who were specifically nominated for this work by their superiors and moved by the Holy Spirit, should volunteer for the work of conversion among the Indians and teach them the Christian faith. They would be free to travel to those parts, if in the opinion of His Majesty or the Royal Council they appeared to be of blameless character and learned enough to undertake work of such importance. It was to be the duty of superiors conscientiously to nominate candidates and to grant licences. Volunteers who had been selected were to be in holy duty bound to undertake the journey and the work for which they had been chosen, following the example of Christ. They received the Holy Father's blessing. On pain of excommunication which would be automatically incurred, nobody was to place obstacles in their way nor obstruct their purpose. This threat of excommunication extended also to seculars and other ecclesiastic authorities, unless they had acted out of ignorance. It extended to all those who tried to hinder the progress of the numerous servants of God who had volunteered for this duty and who were prepared to assist and help with what was most necessary.

From my own experience I can testify what two leading members of a religious order did when I was about to embark for New Spain. They tried to persuade me not to go, though admittedly for religious reasons. One of them caused a companion of mine not to depart; this also happened to others. Since then both the two fathers, though at different times, have been granted good archiepiscopal sees in Spain; alas, neither could take possession of his diocese, for death overtook them before they could do so. Whether or not God punished them for not having allowed others to move to a land where they could render more important services and whether God himself called them, only the Lord himself in His counsel knows, but it is at least a posibility.

In the aforesaid bull, Pope Hadrian lays down that the superiors of orders in Indian locations together with the friars in their care, should have a plain authority, conferred direct by the Holy See and to be exercised in a manner and to the extent necessary for the conversion of the Indians and for the preservation of all other Christians in our Holy Catholic Faith and in obedience to the Church of Rome. This authority they were to use with the assistance of their own friars or those of another mendicant order. The bull authorized and commanded them specifically to undertake this work and to convert the Indians to the faith, but at the same time also to take extra care for other Christians.

It conferred powers which normally were exercised by bishops or which required episcopal personal presence. But the friars were to exercise the powers only if no bishop had been appointed or was available within a reasonable distance. Reasonable distance was defined as any distance exceeding a two-days' journey. The bull also confirmed once more all the indults previously granted by Pope Adrian's predecessors. Together with those conceded later by his successors, they guaranteed the friars free access and activity in the New World.[33]

Chapter 12 : The reception of the Twelve Friars in Mexico City

(In 1523 the Franciscan mission to New Spain took shape under the leadership of Fray Martín de Valencia. The so-called "Twelve Apostles" arrived in

> San Juan de Ulúa on 13 May 1524. At the end of May
> or the beginning of June they passed Tlaxcala, then
> spent another day in Texcoco, and on 17 or 18 June
> they arrived in the city of Mexico.)

When the Governor Don Hernando Cortés received the news of the arrival of these friars, for whom he had applied and whose coming he so much desired, he was overjoyed and cheerfully gave thanks to the Lord for His mercy. He at once ordered members of his staff to depart and meet the party of friars on the road, and this in his name, and also to look after their persons, above all to ensure they had enough food and to prevent any unpleasant incidences. For those regions were by no means safe, having few Spanish colonists, since most of them resided in Mexico City and did not bother with reports of danger.

I have the details of the report which follows from Juan de Villagómez, one of Cortés's attendants.

The friars proceeded towards Mexico City, which from their port of disembarkation is 60 leagues (334.36 km.) distant, on foot, discalced, and with a minimum of comfort. The Governor ordered all the Indian chiefs and princes of the most important places in the environs of the city into his presence, commanding them all to join him in the reception of the ministers of God, who came to teach them the law and God's will and lead them along the path of salvation.

When the servants of God reached Tlaxcala they took a day off to recover from the exertions of the road as well as to see that city, so famous for its large population. On market-day they went to the plaza where most of the people used to congregate to purchase provisions for their families. With amazement they looked on the throng of people, the like and number of whom they had never seen before. With great fervour did they thank God for letting them see this teeming multitude of souls to be converted, longing to start their holy work at once, with this fruitful harvest of souls lying ahead. Being ignorant of the native language, they used sign language to make themselves understood and to convey the idea that they had come to introduce the people to the treasures and glory that dwelt above; they did this by pointing to Heaven. The Indians ran after them like boys following something new. They were amazed to see the friars in their shabby habits, so different from the shining splendour of Spanish soldiers with which they were familiar. And they asked: "What men can be so poor? what sort of dress are they wearing? They are not like those of the Christians of Castille!" They repeatedly used the word *motolinea*. One of the fathers, Toribio de Benavente, asked one of the Spaniards the meaning of the word the Indians kept repeating, and the Spaniard replied: "Father, *motolinea* means 'poor'"; Thereupon Father Toribio said: "Let this be my name for the rest of my life", and from then on he always signed his name as "Toribio Motolinia".

On their arrival in Mexico City, Cortés, accompanied by all Spanish gentlemen and the Indian chiefs who for this reception had been assembled, stepped forward to greet the friars, lowering himself to his knees and kissing the hands of all the brethren. Pedro de Alvarado and all the other Spanish gentlemen and captains did the same. The Indians, witnessing this, followed their example and also kissed the friars' hands.[34]

Chapter 16 : The language problem

Apart from the teaching of children, which kept the friars busy, adult natives too began to memorize the first rudiments of Christian knowledge. Under the direction of their chiefs, men and women met in the larger patios which formed a part of the towns. There they met, for they did not wish to displease or disobey Governor Cortés who had ordered them to do just this. They prayed in Latin, responding to those who taught them, who often were the friars and occasionally even their own children, pupils who had picked everything up quite easily with that kind of facility with which an average intelligent person learns.

This kind of instruction bore little fruit, for the Indians did not understand what was pronounced in Latin. Their idolatry did not stop nor could the friars reproach them nor induce them to abandon their pagan practices, as they could not speak the language. In the early days this left the brethren sad and afflicted; they did not know what to do. Although they wanted to learn the native language, they had nobody to teach them. And the Indians, full of awed reverence for them, did not dare approach them.

It was in this emergency that they appealed to Our Lord, the very fountainhead of goodness and compassion, and they increased their fasting and prayers. They also asked for the intercession of the Holy Virgin, the Mother of God and the angels, whose devotees they were, as well as for the intervention of the Blessed Father St Francis whose sons they were. The Lord suggested to them that the friars should join their pupils in their games, behave like children, and share their conversation; thereby to cultivate linguistic contact with the sincerity and simplicity of their charges. And this came to pass. The friars dropped the grave dignity of their persons and began to play with the children, with small wooden sticks and pebbles, games the children liked, and they reduced the children's reserve and made them talk. The friars always carried paper and ink and, on hearing an Indian verb, they wrote it down together with its meaning. Late in the afternoon they met and, on the basis of their notes, discussed the words they had registered and their meaning in Spanish and agreed on the most adequate translation. Unfortunately it did happen that what yesterday had seemed to them the meaning of a noun, did not appear to be so today.

After having followed this routine for several days, Our Lord comforted his servants in two ways. In the first place, some of the older children began to understand quite well what the padres said and when they saw the friars wished to learn their language, they not only corrected their errors but also asked them many questions, a situation wholly satisfactory to all concerned. The second remedy, which Our Lord granted, turned up in the form of a Spanish woman, a widow, who had two small sons, who played with Indian children and had learnt to speak the native language well. When the friars heard this, they asked the Governor Don Hernando Cortés for one of the boys, and thanks to Cortés's intervention the woman felt honoured and pleased to hand over to the friars one of the small boys, called Alonso. He became another Samuel presented to God in the Temple; from childhood on he laboured incessantly and loyally, never returned to his mother's home nor kept in touch with her, for ever obeying the commands of God's ministers, from his youth on to his very death.

Alonso had a cell in the convent, took his meals and attended mass with the brethren and in everything else he followed their example. He served as interpreter, communicating to the Indians the mysteries of our faith. He became the teacher of the preachers of the Gospel because he taught them the language, staying in each parish where friars lived and worked and instructing all most beneficially.

When coming of age, Alonso took the habit of the Order and continued to work up to his old age. You will find details of this and a biography in Book V, Chapter 48. He is known as Fray Alonso de Molina.[35]

Chapter 24 : The Holy zeal of the boys of Tlaxcala

When in the first year of their activities in the City of Tlaxcala the friars began to enrol the sons of princes and lords to teach them, those who served in the temples of Satan had not ceased to serve and look after the idols; they never stopped to persuade the ordinary people not to desert their own gods, for, they said, they alone were true and catered for all their needs; the god of the friars on the contrary did not do this, however much they and their disciples claimed this in words and in sermons. And to prove this, they dressed one of them in the insignia of one of their gods, called Ometochtli,[36] believed to be the god of pulque, another Bacchus. This person walked into the market place, pretending to be most wild and awesome. As a token of his ferocity he carried in his mouth some black flint pieces which they used as knives, and in this masquerade he circulated in the market in the presence of a large crowd who were mystified by this novelty; for only on rare occasions did a priest leave the temples thus attired, but when he did, he received much respectful attention and reverence, and they scarcely dared look him in the face.

On this occasion the children who were taught in the monastery arrived to wash themselves in the river; to reach it they had cross the market place. When they saw the large crowd surrounding the demon, or rather his image, they asked who he was. Some replied: "Our god Ometochtli." The children said: "He is no god, he is a devil who lies and misleads you!" In the very centre of the market stood a cross, and when the children passed it, they showed their respect in the manner they had been taught. As they were many, they stopped there for a while to allow stragglers to catch up with them. It was then that the man masquerading as a god went up to them, increasingly annoyed. He chided them and said they would have to die soon, for they had annoyed him by leaving their homes and joining the new God and Santa María, for that was the name of the cathedral of Tlaxcala. Some of the older youths replied, courageously and daringly, that they were not afraid, that he was a liar and that they were not going to die as he had predicted. There was, they said, only one God, the maker of heaven and earth and everything else; he, the masked man, was no god but a demon or his image.

The masked man protested that he was a god and, abusing them in his attempt to frighten the children, his own anger grew. By this time a large crowd had gathered around them, awaiting the outcome of the argument. And when the man persisted in pretending to be a god and the children became more and more sure he was nothing more than the image of a devil, one of them bent down to collect a stone, saying to his classmates: "Let us get rid of this devil! May God help us!" Saying this he threw the stone at him, while his mates did likewise. At first the man tried to face them, but he faltered and took to his heels when all the boys bombarded him and hit him. It thus happened that, for his sins, he stumbled. Hardly had he fallen when they found him dead and covered with stones. This left the boys triumphant and in some glory, as if they had accomplished some great deed, and they said: "Today the people of Tlaxcala will see that the man was not a god but a villain and a liar. God and the Holy Virgin are good and they have helped us to slay Satan."

When this had been accomplished and the unfortunate madman had perished, the general impression prevailed that they had not killed a man but a veritable devil. And as occurs in war with a battle won, the victors felt full of joy, the defeated downhearted and broken, the latter in this case being the servants of and believers in idols. The faithful were overjoyed. Many of the pagan priests now arrived in order to lay hands on the boys, but they failed, for they remained aghast and in panic when they saw the corpse of the one who had gone forth to frighten the people.

The boys entered the monastery, proud of themselves and in high spirits, convinced they had slain the devil. The friars did not understand what was going on; they called an Indian who had come from the market place and asked him. When they heard what had happened they intended to punish the boys, and they asked them who had killed the man. They said, all of them;

they had acted in unison; that creature had not been a man but a demon trying to become a god; that he had done his hardest to curse, and if possible, even to kill them; that he had been prevented from doing so by God and the Virgin Mary, who had saved them from his hands and punished him according to his deserts.

Chapter 31 : The frugality and abstinence of the friars

In general terms we have already mentioned the extreme poverty and conditions of penance in which these fortunate brethren, our predecessors, lived, who by means of their sermons implanted in the minds of the Indians the knowledge of the Gospels. We are their successors in this sacred work and are in honour bound to follow in their footsteps. In their honour of memory we shall now cite some of the many witnesses of their abstinence and penitential frugality. There are many and even I can remember only some few of the examples.

Fray Diego de Amonte [who according to our author arrived with the second boatload of Franciscans; see Bk. V(1), Ch. 32] used to tell that in the beginning when they had no cabbage or other vegetables, which are plentiful now, they boiled wild camomile which, before it ripens is full of seeds as bitter as medlar, something hardly digestible even if one is starving. They had no oil, fat or butter to prepare vegetables. Others, years later, managed to roast them over a fire. At mealtimes they used to go to the plazas or some Indian market, begging for the sake of God and asking for some maize tortillas and chili. Sometimes they were given small fruit and they ate it. The natives did not respect the friars any less for rejecting almost everything and for suffering for the love of God. There was certainly a glut of chickens, but on the few occasions when they received them as a gift, they ate them but only after having divided a hen into ever so many tiny portions, too small even to be tasted by a friar, and I also know that two friars who always worked together shared it in this fashion. And when in the permissible periods of the year they ate chicken, one had to last an entire week; they rationed it in the following way: on Sundays they boiled it and consumed the giblets, in particular the neck, head, liver and stomach. During the next days they fried each day a quarter of the meat. They never had an evening meal, following a general rule in the province, except on Sundays when they were permitted to take a snack. As a consequence of such frugality and lack of food they often collapsed during their visits and on the road.

In spite of these hardships they continued with their teaching, sermons and visits, and to a much greater extent than they do today. The Lord gave them great strength and comforted them, for man does not live from bread alone! They regarded the consumption of wine an offence, not only because of the high cost of the imported beverage but also because in New Spain it has the effect of fire and it overheats the body. This fact obviously compelled the brethren to look for some other kinds of innocuous drinks, such as water boiled with the leaves of certain trees. I have seen this done, with my own eyes; Fray Francisco de Soto, one of the first "Twelve" said that the local "wine" [i.e. pulque] should be sold by apothecaries and be dispensed to the sick. When Father Ciudad Rodrigo, as superior of the convent of Mexico, refused to accept a jug of wine which the saintly Archbishop Zumárraga sent him as a festive present for the friars, he returned it with thanks, saying that because he loved his friars so much, he requested him not to allow any relaxation which would inevitably lead to the growth of bad habits. That great servant of God, Brother Martín de Valencia, reproached the same bishop when one day they were travelling along a road and the bishop produced a leather winebag to dispense a few drops to the worn-out and thoroughly fatigued friars. The brethren did not even consent to harbour two small jars of wine on the premises, except a tiny one containing wine for the celebration of mass.

A similar poverty reigned in respect of clothing. Fray Diego de Almonte, speaking of himself, said that the habit in which he had arrived from Spain was so torn that he could no longer hold the pieces together. He made his school children carefully pull the threads from the rags and collect them in balls of woollen fibre. Some Indian women would then interweave them with cotton and produce for him a new garment, loose-fitting and at the lowest imaginable cost. This is what Fray Diego did for there was no wool to be had. All suffered from near-nakedness, and yet remained strong in their principles and resolution. The friars who arrived from Spain did not ask for any other clothes than those in which they stood. Habits wore out fairly quickly, and in the end all they wore were cotton garments, dyed brown.

While on this subject I would like to mention the efforts of an Indian chief who successfully tried to keep his friars clothed, and tell you how he and his servants actually managed to produce sackcloth. This chief, called Don Martín, lord of the town of Guacachula, was most devoted to the brethren and on the most friendly terms with them. When he saw the threadbareness of their habits, he took pity on them. He knew that a craftsman had arrived in Mexico City who specialized in the manufacture of sackcloth. He actually had a monopoly, and whatever he produced he sold at once. The Indian ordered some of his retainers to go to Mexico and to enter the service of this manufacturer; they should secretly observe the process of manufacture and return once they were in possession of the industrial secret. They did this, learning clandestinely the process of weaving and obtaining a good knowledge too of the machinery and tools involved. They discussed among themselves what they picked up. In a short time they knew everything except they could not handle warp. Yet even that they learnt shortly afterwards and, without taking leave of the Spanish craftsman, they packed up a bundle of the cloth, a vara [83.6 cm.] in length and returned to Guacachula. There they began to weave and produced the cloth for the friars' habits.[37]

(The author continues supplying further examples of the friars' frugality.)

Chapter 41 : Indian confession in their pagan period

In their pagan days the Indians in some part of New Spain practised a kind of confession of their sins which they addressed to their gods. Twice yearly they would go into a corner of their house, or in the temple, or even in the hills or to some special springs, choosing whatever place suited their devotional needs best. There they would display signs of very great contrition, shedding copious tears, joining their hands as if in great affliction and contorting their fingers; they also made wry faces while confessing their errors and sins. During this exercise which lasted days, they never laughed nor did anything pleasurable, but they immersed themselves in feelings of sadness, regret, and misery.

Sometimes they confessed their sins to healers or sorcerers when asking for some remedy or advice. When a healer was called to treat a patient whose condition was not serious, he would prescribe some herbs and such like, but if the sick person suffered from a dangerous and serious disease, he said: "You are guilty of a sin." He pestered and worried the patient by repeating these words so insistently that he compelled him to confess, even something he might have committed years before. Sin they considered the principal cause of illness, and confession, they said, helped to expel sin from the body and to restore a patient to health.[38]

Chapter 50 : The friars clash with the authorities

The Spaniards had become masters of vast estates inhabited by a dense native population, wholly subject and obedient to any order they gave; the Spaniards lived without restraint, each doing what he fancied and indulging in every imaginable kind of vice. They treated the Indians with such severity and cruelty that no book would be large enough to present a detailed story of all their misdeeds. The tribute demanded was usually so excessive that when the Indians could not meet the demands, they sold their land and their children to native usurers, the children reverting to the status of slaves. Tribute payments never ended, and when the natives could not sell their property, they left their villages which remained empty or on the brink of depopulation. A reduction of tribute alone would remedy this situation. In a district some forty or fifty leagues from Mexico City the natives had to serve their masters, the *encomenderos*, for weeks on end, and all the time they had to provide them with all their needs: chickens, maize, fruit, fish, cacao, firewood, horse-fodder and whatever else they demanded, while the women worked in the kitchens preparing tortillas. For the construction of houses, which resembled veritable palaces, all the lime and wood had to be carried over distances of some forty or fifty leagues.

The friars, seeing that these abuses continued without anything being done, and desirous that the Indians should love our faith and the Christian religion, preached against these sins and vices so openly committed, and with good Christian fervour condemned them publicly. When those in power, who themselves were guilty of these or often even worse crimes, such as imposing slave status on freemen and free women, saw this, they immediately reacted as if the friars had been dangerous enemies; they cut their alms-giving and set out to defame and besmirch their name in public; they did them as much harm as they could. As they feared the friars might inform the King, they immediately applied all means at their disposal to obstruct the friars' communications, verbal or written, with the outside world. They decreed that all letters written by the friars would be subject to censorship. They also searched the ships and turned the cargo upside down, looking for messages. And if this were not enough, in their attempt to prevent news of their misdeeds reaching Spain, they tried to stop communications from the sufferers themselves leaking out. As the miscreants were officials and secretaries, they were able to manufacture false information, accusing the bishops and the friars of ugly offences which in truth existed solely in the writers' imagination.

When the libellous information reached Spain, the Emperor Charles V was absent in one of his other kingdoms, and the very Christian Empress, who acted as regent, on reading the accusations, could not think it possible for the good friars, who had gone overseas, to have committed contemptible crimes, particularly not the first bishop, Juan de Zumárraga, for they were all virtuous and worthy men. More and more news arrived, but no excuse or defence from the friars themselves. The Council of the Indies was most concerned and disturbed and felt that something had to be done. The Almighty, who sometimes permits such things to happen, desirous of alleviating the suffering of the friars, chose a Basque sailor who arrived from Castile and knew the situation in which the bishop found himself. The sailor offered to take a letter safely to Spain and deliver it into the Empress's hands. This he did, for when the bishop had given him the letters, the sailor hid them secretly in a buoy, something you can read in the biography of Fray Juan de Zumárraga.

In the meantime the judges and governors of New Spain, bent on harming the friars, caused a thousand affronts and insults to the Indians and interfered with the friars' prerogative of jurisdiction in cases of eclesiastic offences, and even with the teaching of the Gospel. The crisis reached such a climax that Fray Luis de Fuensalida, custodian of the Franciscan Order, seeing that the friars had been deprived of their powers and the ability to spread the word of God properly, ordered the brethren to cease their teaching, as the Audiencia [Supreme Court] had ordered them to do.

At this very moment a messenger arrived stating that the bishop had received two letters from the Empress. The judges of the Audiencia now trembled. Shortly afterwards the bishop arrived, carrying two letters, one addressed to him and the other to the friars, and with tears of joy the letters were read and thanks given to God. The custodian wrote to all the superiors and guardians of the convents, countermanding his previous order and commanding them to resume their work with all possible energy, for the Lord had not forgotten them.

Within a few months a new governor and new judges arrived, more righteous and Christian-minded, who favoured the service of God and the growth of the new Church which had suffered from so much affliction. The previous governor, deprived of his office, was imprisoned in a public gaol under very harsh conditions, while the guilty judges were treated harshly and with scorn, forever after discredited.[39]

Chapter 56 : How the natives love St Francis and his brethren
From the very start of their conversion the Indians honoured and loved St Francis and the friars, for they instinctively felt the holiness of these apostolic men, the first missionaries. Even when they could not understand their language, they judged them from their appearance. They placed an enormous faith in the Franciscan habit as such. They asked for friars in villages where they had none and when, as a consequence of the shortage of Franciscans, they were offered friars of another order, they used to say: "Father, if you have no priest to take up residence in our town and to teach us the catechism and the sacraments, do not bother; we shall trust God's mercy. Give us just a single habit of St Francis. We shall on Sundays and feastdays raise it up on

a pole. We hope that God will endow it with a voice to preach to us and thus leave us perfectly contented." There were very few who did not dedicate small children to the Father St Francis. The children wore the Franciscan habit, and this as a result of a vow for the duration of an entire year, some even until they became adolescent. It was a real experience to see the events which took place on the eve of St Francis [3 October] in all the houses of the Order, especially in large towns. There the first services would be attended by more than 800 of the faithful, sometimes by a 1,000 children with their mothers, relatives and friends, also godparents who as a token of their respect wore special dresses or belts to be blessed, also carrying candles of white wax. Many brought offerings of bread, fruit and things to demonstrate their devotion.

Once the solemn part of the feast was over and they had been blessed, they took off the special clothes they had worn, for they were unaccustomed to the close fit. They raised their voices and they sounded like just a mass of goats or sheep. The same thing happened on the day of the feast of the saint [4 October]. After mass the festivities went on for another week, for not all had been able to attend on the exact dates. It happened that in the course of the year, because of illness or some other reason, some had to cease wearing the habit of St Francis.

Adults, even those most devoted to St Francis, did not wear the cord, certainly not before the foundation of the confraternity instituted by Pope Sixtus V. Since then many Indians wear the cord. It was the Indian women in labour who from the very beginning of their conversion, in an ardent spirit of devotion and faith, asked for the cord of St Francis, and it is in this context that Our Lord has shown much compassion, seeing the horror of pregnant women spending a day or more in labour. The women sent to the monastery for a cord, and, as soon as they had received it, they gave birth and were out of danger. I have seen this remedy applied for more than forty years, and the cord has always been effective.

It is also quite common to see in our houses, in the porter's lodge or hung up in the refectory, an old cord, cast off by the friars. I believe that another reason why the Indians hold this saint in such esteem is that originally in this land, at the end of September, or the beginning of October, it began to hail, often on St Francis's Day itself or on the eve; this was an annual, most cruel, event. Our Lord has since brought it about that thanks to the Saint's intercession this damaging event has ceased to occur.[40]

Chapter 56 : St Francis works a miracle

In a village called Atacubaya, a league distant from Mexico City, a boy named Ascencio grew up, son of a quaryman or mason called Domingo; he had reached the age of seven or eight years. Domingo, his wife, and children were all greatly devoted to St Francis and his friars. Whenever a friar passed them, they greeted him and readily shared with him what little they had.

The boy Ascencio fell ill, and as his condition worsened, the parents went to their village church, dedicated to the wound-scars of St Francis, and there humbly asked the saint to intercede on their son's behalf. But as the sickness got still worse, the parents visited the saint in the church once more, supplicating him, in all modesty, to take pity on them. But since the Lord meant to exalt his saint with a manifest miracle, he allowed the child to die, one morning after sunrise.

Despite their son's death the distressed parents continued to pray to St Francis whom they trusted with the most sincere conviction. In the afternoon they placed the remains into a shroud and made preparations for his burial later on. Before they shrouded him, many persons saw him cold, rigid and dead. So they got ready to take him to the church. Meanwhile the friars had never faltered in their faith and confidence in the glorious Father St Francis and expected that God would grant him the boy's life. They began to pray and devoutly invoked St Francis when the boy suddenly began to move; he rapidly loosened the shroud and took it off. The dead boy had come back to life at the very hour of Vespers.

The many who attended the funeral service remained bewildered, while the boy's parents were greatly consoled. The news was at once imparted to the friars of San Francisco El Grande of Mexico City, and the famous Fray Pedro de Gante, head of the teaching establishment, arrived. When he and his escort saw the boy alive and cured, after having ascertained from the parents and other trustworthy persons what had happened, he asked the entire population to gather, and in front of them made the father confirm that his son had returned to life, thanks to the intercession and excellence of the glorious and seraphic Father St Francis.

The news of the miracle spread to all the neighbouring districts, and it had an edifying and invigorating effect, fortifying our holy faith, for in this land they had never heard of anybody returning from the dead. It persuaded many to become believers in the marvellous miracles performed by our Redeemer and his saints, of which they read and heard from their preachers.

BOOK IV

Chapter 1 : Praise for Bartolomé de Las Casas

While praising the memory of all those who loyally laboured in the service of the conversion of the Indians, it will be only fair to mention the members of the other orders who have also toiled and contributed much to Christianity. One such was the Bishop of Chiapas, Don Fray Bartolomé de Las Casas of the Order of the Blessed St Dominic, who, before taking the habit, had been a secular priest in the island of Española. With pious Christian zeal he began to shed tears, clamouring for divine clemency. He informed their Catholic Majesties, shortly before their deaths, of the massive destruction and liquidation of the natives of the islands. After having become a friar and after having been raised to the dignity of an episcopal seat, he renounced the see to become "Protector of the Indians", residing at the royal court. He acted as advisor for a period of twenty-two years, suffering many setbacks, much hardship and opposition. Some of his own Dominicans, but more so the sons of St Francis resident in New Spain, kept him informed of the vexations and harm suffered by the recently converted natives. His ceaseless endeavours led to the mitigation of many abuses and, in particular, to the liberation of Indians treated as slaves. Their slavery ceased from then on, and all the Indians became freemen. He wrote a great deal, in Latin and in the vernacular, pointing out that our Spaniards had an obligation to defend and help the natives, and all his writings are based on rational thought and on divine and human laws. He was exceedingly well read and a very learned man.

I am fully convinced that he will enjoy special glory in heaven, wearing the most precious crown in return for the deprivations, hunger, and thirst he endured as a most zealous and persevering advocate, right up to his death. He suffered for the glory and love of God in a never-ending battle for the poor and the unfortunate . . .[41]

Chapter 12 : Traditional native skills

They had good sculptors who worked the stone with flint tools, for they lacked iron, and they managed this work as effectively as the best artist with a stonemason's hammer of steel in our land of Castile, as you can still see in the figures protruding from the cemented surfaces of some of the corners of principal buildings in Mexico, though they no longer come up to the high standards of the past.

Carpenters and engravers worked wood with copper tools but they did not produce such interesting objects as the stonemasons did. Lapidaries worked precious stones and polished and shaped them into whatever figure or form was wanted, and this by applying some special kind of sand, only known to them, still in use now, though you no longer find precious stones among Indians.

Silversmiths did not possess metal hammers, but by placing the silver between two flay stones they managed to produce silver-plate.

They had good painters who reproduced natural objects, particularly birds, trees, animals, and such like with which they covered the walls of the royal palaces. But the representations of the human form lacked beauty and encouraged ugliness, for they also expressed likenesses of their horrible gods. They were trained to paint that way, and their gods appeared to them to have bodies expressing their sins and the darkness in which their souls dwelt. Since they have become Christians and have seen Flemish and Italian paintings, they have learnt to cover every retable with copies. From any material, wood, bone, or clay, they produce tiny and curious objects which have become popular in Spain. They also make crucifixes from reed stalks, so well-shaped, proportioned and devotional as if they were made of wax; they could not bettered!

From clay their potters produced eating and drinking utensils, all painted and of excellent shape, though glazing was not known. They picked glazing up very quickly from the first ceramic worker who arrived from Spain, however much he tried to keep the secret of his craft from them. They also made vessels from calabashes, the material being much harder and different from ours, for it was the product of a tropical tree. They painted these vessels and still do so today, covering the surfaces with a diversity of figures, and in splendid colours. The paint is so well integrated with the surface that even if the vessel is immersed in water for a hundred years, the painting would not be effaced and lost. They make cups and goblets of the same material and in the same style, elegant, and most beautiful to behold.[42]

Clothing, especially that made for the kings, and the vestments of the priests, consisted mainly of cotton, white, black, and embellished with an array of different colours, with the fabric itself either thick or thin according to the purpose of the garment, often even resembling Moorish gauze. They also manufactured material made of rabbit-skins interwoven with cotton, much favoured by the aristocracy and, when tailored, resembling Irish cloaks; they protected them from the cold and were very warm and soft, but also had the appearance of a fine artistic product.

Tanners cured the skin of deer, jaguars, pumas, and other animals; they prepared them in a magnificent manner, both as skins and furs, white, red, blue, black, yellow, all smooth, and today they still manufacture gloves in that manner. Apart from common footwear which consisted of maguey fibre from the stalks of that plant, they created for the royalty and their nobles delicately shaped, smooth shoes, either of maguey or cotton, some painted or even gilded.[43]

(Mendieta continues to comment at great length on feathercraft and the manufacture of flint or obsidian knives.)

Chapter 13 : The Indians learn European trades and skills

The first and only college in New Spain, designed to teach a whole range of necessary skills and knowledge, open not only to those employed or earmarked for the employment by the Church, but also for laymen, was the Chapel of San José, adjoining the monastery of St Francis in the City of Mexico, where Father Pedro de Gante resided for many years, the first and busiest teacher of the Indians.[44] Not content with running a large infant school in which he taught the Christian faith as well as reading, writing and singing, he arranged, for adolescents, instruction in the trades, the arts and crafts of the Spaniards, of which their parents and forebears had been ignorant, and all this with the aim of perfecting their own traditional skills. For this purpose he set aside, at the back of the chapel, some rooms; there he assembled his trainees and taught them the most common European skills first: tailoring, cobbling, painting, and such like. Later he switched to trades, requiring higher skill. Obviously there were tremendous difficulties at the outset: many of those nearest to his trainees had died, for the war had just come to an end, and the natives, with so many of their friends and relatives dead and their city in ruins, were perplexed and still stunned. All this made their introduction of Spanish techniques and the more advanced methods exceedingly difficult. But they began to gain confidence in acquiring simpler techniques. Many of them acted like monkeys, imitating the actions of others they observed. Yet in a relatively short time they mastered the skills even more efficiently than their instructor had expected.

Some enterprising craftsmen, newly arrived from Spain, had at first a monopoly, but the Indians very soon upset them with their patent astuteness, their ingenuity and quest for perfection. I have already in my Book III mentioned a case of "trade espionage" affecting a sackcloth manufacturer. A gold sheet-metal-worker, the first to arrive, meant to keep his practices secret, by saying it would take a man six or seven years to learn the trade from him. But the Indians were not going to wait that long; instead they secretly picked up all the details of these particular skills, even counting the number of hammer blows and how to wield this tool, how to use moulds, etc. And before a year had passed, they were able to produce beaten gold. They had even "borrowed" a small handbook from him, which he had not missed until they returned it to him.

Something similar happened in the embossed leather trade, when the Spanish expert craftsman did his utmost to conceal from the Indians the secrets of his craft, especially how to give the leather a golden or silvery colour. When the Indians became aware of his attempts to protect his trade secrets, they decided to scrutinize all the materials; they then took a small pinch of every substance involved and went to see a friar and said: "Padre, please tell us where they sell these substances. We would like to acquire them, for that Spaniard hides them from us. We wish to produce embossed leather and give it the same colours of gold and silver as created by Spanish experts." The friar (most likely Fray Pedro de Gante) concurred with this mischief and told them where to purchase the materials, and soon they produced their own embossed leather.

When the Indians intended to copy saddles (a Spaniard had just opened his workshop) they tried to ascertain what materials went to the making of saddle-trees and bows and other constituents. The saddlemaker, following general custom, had a saddle hanging on the door of his house. They waited until he went to have a meal and seized the saddle in order to copy it. They did the same on the following day, but this time the saddler saw it and became apprehensive of his products falling into the hands of Indians - as had happened to other craftsmen, whose products were now peddled in the streets. And this is precisely what happened, for within a week Indians were selling saddles in the markets. They even went to his workshop, asking him whether he wanted to buy some of their saddles. At this stage, rage seized him, for he had been a monopolist, free to fix prices, but in the face of the new Indian competition he had to reduce his charges.

Another trade they soon took up and perfected was the manufacture of bells; they mastered everything required: size, thickness, handles, rims, and even the correct consistency of the metal. Their foundries produced numerous bells, large, small, all neat and of excellent tone quality.

They were also taught the art of embroidery by a saintly lay brother of Italian origin, but born in Spain, named Father Daniel, whom I shall mention in my Book V [Ch. 25], which deals with the provinces of Michoacán and Jalisco, where he lived and died, leaving many decorated articles behind, not expensive but curious and most attractive, all made by hand and by his Indian pupils.

The acquaintance with Spanish techniques also led to a perfection of skills the natives had cultivated before the conquest. Stonemasons and sculptors had worked without iron producing masterpieces, but now, in control of pickaxes, stonecutter hammers and other iron implements and acquainted with the works created by Spanish artists, they made enormous advances. They now produced proper arches of all types, portals and windows, sculptured masks, and they built many fine churches and residences for the Spaniards.[45]

What they had not learnt was to make vaults. When the first one was built by a Spanish craftsman and stonemason for the chapel of the old church of San Francisco in Mexico, many of the Indians were amazed when they saw the vault and simply could not imagine how it possibly stayed in place without scaffolding. They did not venture to walk beneath the vault, but they lost their fear when they realized how firm the ceiling was. Shortly afterwards the Indians constructed the vaults of two small chapels which still form part of the cathedral of Tlaxcala. Since then they have built the roofs of numerous fine churches, also in the tropical parts.

Their carpenters used to cover the palaces of their kings with fine wood; they also produced much else, but today their work has changed, for they have acquired proper carpentry and joinery, as well as workshop practices, enabling them to produce anything Spanish tradesmen create, as well as works of masonry and architecture.

To sum up: it has to be taken as a general rule, that all noteworthy, worthwhile artefacts, in whatever trade or craft, found in the Indies, or at least in New Spain, are the works of Indians. The Spanish masters tell the Indians what they want done, and the Indians carry the instructions out to perfection.

(Chapter 14 deals mainly with native advances in oral and instrumental music.)

Chapter 22 : Native attempts to lead communal religious lives

In his letter to the Romans (Romans X) the glorious Apostle St Paul states that in the divine presence no differences exist between Jews and Greeks or the Scythian barbarians; nor do they exist between Spaniard and Indian, for He is the Creator and Lord of all, bestowing wealth and power upon both, and He favours one or the other when they invoke His holy name. And the Lord pronounces this in even greater brevity by saying that it is the Holy Spirit which inspires sacred desires and longings in those who wish to receive Him: I am stressing this, for although some Spaniards try to keep the Indians in a low and despised human and social condition, many Indians have, in fact, by their actions displayed contempt for the world and expressed the desire to follow Jesus Christ with the utmost fervour and in a frame of mind that I, poor Spaniard and Franciscan friar, would wish for myself in the observance and fulfilment of the evangelic life I have professed to God. From the many I have met, I shall now select some to bring them into sharp relief for those who constantly run the Indians down and speak ill of them.

An Indian, a resident of Cholula named Baltasar, was filled with the spirit of God to such extent that he was no longer content with trying to save his own soul. Circulating in neighbouring towns and villages like Tepeaca, Tecali, Tecamachalco, and Guatinchan, he tried to attract as many Indians as possible to his beliefs and devotion. He searched in the mountainous country in the vicinity of the volcano and the Sierra Nevada of Tecamachalco for a suitable location to execute his plans, namely to devote himself to God by leading a quiet and solitary life. He enrolled all who wished to join him, accepting also men with families, women and children, to live in the place he had selected. It was situated between the two rivers which rise in the snow-covered sierra, one large, the other smaller. The large one formed a formidable gorge, which, to reach from his location, required wooden ladders. Here he created a community with an appreciable number of settlers, and he named it "Chocoman" which means "tears of penance". He insisted on their decent behaviour, and with common consensus he formulated certain laws and ordinances, regulating their lives and prayers. Forty years have since passed. But I remember they acquired a reputation of sanctity and were called *beatos* [blessed], and their devotion and humility were much admired. It went so far that the women of the community on no account looked another man in the face!

Fray Juan de Ribas, one of the twelve early arrivals [see Bk. V, Ch. 24] loved these Indians and on many occasions went to lend them spiritual support and to strengthen their resolve. Thanks to his influence they maintained the rigour of penance and continued the holy practices they had started. They asked the authorities for one or two friars, to take charge of their welfare and in particular their belief, so that they would not weaken in the course of time, but the petition fell upon deaf ears, for at that time larger communities asked for similar assistance and failed to obtain it. What is likely to happen is that some cleric, perhaps a vicar of neighbouring community, will take charge of the religious group. He may be a priest, thirty years or less old, and by that time the Indians will most likely have reverted to the common mode of living.

Chapter 23 : Why natives are not permitted to take the habit

You could ask: "Brother, you say that in general these Indians are well disposed and by nature inclined to be good Christians; you have also given individual examples of Indians who have entered into the spirit of God, have expressed the wish to serve Him, readiness to renounce the world and to embrace the religious life. If this is so, why then do you not give them the habit, not just that of a lay brother, but even that of a fully-fledged priest? Did not, in the primitive church, newly converted gentiles and Jews become priests and bishops? This seems to be an excellent means for the promotion of conversion and solid Christianity in the entire race, for these men would also be able to preach and administer the sacraments in their native language in all their forms and complete perfection! Would not the natives prefer to receive their religious instruction from the mouths of fellow natives rather than from strangers?"

To this we have to give a brief and concise reply, admitting that in the primitive church and even still later, this actually happened, because God worked miracles for the recently concerted; they were saints and voluntarily suffered martyrdom for the name of Jesus Christ. Moreover in those days, the church, full of the light of the Holy Spirit was still learning from many setbacks and relapses experienced with new Christians. It was then that the Vicars of Christ laid down that nobody should be professed and ordained, unless he belonged to the fourth generation in a pagan's lineage, and this rule also applies to us.

To this I have to add something. There is not the slightest reason to assume in any way that the Indians want or ever wanted to return to the nauseating customs and rites of their heathen past. This may well be one of the reasons for the refusal to grant to descendants of pagans the privilege of the habit and the priesthood. Yet there is another reason for the refusal to grant the descendants of pagans ordination, and this has absolutely nothing to do with the constancy or otherwise of their Christian convictions. It is a natural trait of most of the Indians (and in this they differ from other nations, except perhaps from the Greeks) in that they lack the ability to command and to direct; they prefer to be ordered and told what to do. Being possessed of humility and a spirit of subjection, which I have already described, they would become vain and cave in under the pressures of high office. They are not made to be masters but to be disciples, not capable of being prelates but only to be members of the crowd and servants, albeit the best in the world. For that role they are wellnigh perfect. Meanwhile, I, a poor specimen, not much good for anything, supported only by my king's favours, have to make sure they do not relapse or disobey. And I do this with only a handful of companions, governing a province of 50,000 Indians, keeping it in as good an order as a convent.[46]

Chapter 27 : Religious experiences of the Indians

On the Friday before Palm Sunday in 1537 there died a certain Benito, an Indian of Cholula. He had been well and in good spirits when he went to confess in the church of Tlaxcala. Two days later he fell ill in the house of a native neighbour, at some distance from the monastery. Feeling that his end was near, he walked to the monastery. Father Toribio Motolinia, who knew him well because he had been one of his pupils, was shocked, for the man's face looked like that of one not belonging to this world. He asked what he had come for, and Benito said he wished to receive the sacrament of reconciliation, for he was dying. After the confession and after having rested a little, he said that he had had a vision of the pains of hell; this had caused him terrible fear, terror, and torment. Even remembering the experience made him shaking and horrified. He said that facing the terrible place his soul had called out to God, asking for his mercy, and, in immediate response, he had been raised up to a place of pleasure and delight, while the angel who carried him had said: "Benito, God has mercy on you! Go and confess your sins and prepare yourself for whither God's clemency will take you!" Father Toribio says he was most astonished to see one so weak and fragile being able to take to the road. He never doubted the vision. Benito died when he had finished telling his story.[47]

A similar experience is related of another Indian, Juan, a resident of the village of Santa Ana, a league distant from Tlaxcala. Juan was responsible for the registration of children born in his village and for rounding them up on Sundays, to take them to classes or have them baptized. When he fell ill, suffering from a disease which eventually led to his death, his soul wandered off, and he was carried by some Negroes along a dreary and difficult road to a dark locality, a place of torment. And when those who carried him were about to cast him into the pit, he cried out in a loud voice, almost as if to protect his rights: "Santa María, My Lady, why am I here? Do I not collect the children and take them to be baptized to the house of God? Have I not rendered service to God and you, My Lady? Santa María, please help me, relieve me from these torments and pains so that I can do penance for my sins. Holy Virgin, help me to escape and protect me from these negroes!" At once liberated from this danger and encouraged by the favour shown him by the Queen of compassion, his soul returned to his body which, so his mother said, had been left for dead all the time. He related additional frightening and extraordinary incidents and pledged a major change in his life. He confessed and promised to live a good life. He died from his illness.

In Ahuacatlán, a place in Jalisco, lived a decent Indian, named Pedro (I do not know if he is still alive) and there he served as interpreter, assisting the brethren in their religious teaching. This Indian was found dead, and he himself affirms that he really had expired. They placed him into a shroud to take him to be buried, and his wife and children wept for him, when two Franciscan friars appeared. One of them was Fray Alonso de Cebreros, who had died as superior of the local monastery, a man of immaculate reputation and among the Indians a tireless teacher of the truth. I do not know who the second friar was. Father Alonso spoke to his companion and said: "Let us preserve this man, for he is the friars' interpreter, and they need him; he also has a wife and small children." Having said this, they vanished. The Indian rose and recovered from his illness; he has lived the life of a good and devout Christian.

In the village of Topoyanco or Santa Agueda, lived a most devout Indian who on every occasion, when friars visited the place, came out to greet them with expressions of pleasure and showing particular love for Fray Rodrigo de Bienvenida. When this brother arrived on a visit, the Indian went, as usual, out onto the road to receive him, but this time he was extraordinarily weak. The superior asked him what ailed him and the Indian told him that he had been very sick, so ill in fact that for two or three days members of his household thought him dying or dead. It had been during this interval that he had been carried off to the seat of judgement, where demons tried to rob him of his soul, while angels defended it; that in the end the Apostle Santiago [St James the Greater], whom he had always held in special regard, had forced the demons to flee. The Indian regained consciousness and recovered, though the experience had left him seriously weakened.

A married Indian woman went to see a friar with a complaint against her husband, who kept a mistress and treated his wife badly. When the husband heard this, he beat her up and injured her so severely that she expected to die; she had herself carried to the monastery for her confession. It was late and the friar on duty was tired; in any case, it looked as if she was not quite as sick as she made out, and he said he would confess her on the following day. When she returned to her home the Lord Jesus Christ and His Holy Mother appeared to her, and Our Lady asked Her Son's help for this Indian woman. Our Lord said that St Peter should come, and he arrived indeed. He laid hands on her, who happened to be a devotee of the saint, and he cured her. He also informed her that in a number of days she would die. On the following morning she went to see the friar, to whom she told all that had happened. This friar, Fray Juan de Ayora, was himself a man of apostolic quality and an example to others. When superior in Michoacán he resigned his office and with two Carmelites went to the Philippines to resume, in his old age, labours in the Lord's vineyard, and there he died. He himself told me the story.

Another Indian, a chief's wife from Culiacán, died from some disease. She had already been dead for more than twenty-four hours and placed into a shroud. When they wanted to place her onto the bier to take her to the cemetery, she stirred and tore the shroud. She told the astonished party of mourners that she had appeared before the seat of judgement of the Lord Jesus Christ, who had expressed his dissatisfaction with the entire province and who commanded her soul to return to her body to tell the people to listen to the word of God as preached by the friars and to follow their exhortations. She had been spared for this very mission through the mercy and compassion of the Lord. But she would have to die soon. This she did two days later. Fray Gaspar Rodríguez, the lady's confessor, confirms that she was an exemplary Christian and free from vice.

A sick Indian was taken to the church in Xochimilco to be confessed. Friar Diego de Sande arrived to hear his confession. He saw that the man was dying (he had lost the power of speech) and the friar reproached those who carried him for not having brought him earlier. But the sick man immediately opened his mouth and said: "Padre, it had not been my intention to confess. I did not allow them to take me here because I could not be bothered with you. But last night, when the bells signalled Matins, the pains, caused by my illness, prevented me from sleeping; I was alone, for my wife slept in the adjoining room. I saw the heaven open and enter my room. I beheld Our Lord Jesus Christ crucified, portrayed in the same style as in our church, and he said to me in great wrath: 'Sinner! Let me tell you that you will die tomorrow, and your sins call for a severe judgement. But because I take pity on you I shall pardon your sins, provided you confess them all!' And, Padre, this is the reason for my being so late for my confession!" The friar confessed him and the Indian expired.

(In Chapter 28 Mendieta presents cases of apparitions and visions.)

Chapter 33 : The loss of social discipline among the natives

Among the damage done to the Indians in their new way of life their contact with the Spaniards is one of the most prominent facets. I cannot list every single factor and can mention only a few which stick in my mind. Those Indians, of course, who are persistent in the service of God and have strong souls, avoid dubious contacts or control their behaviour. It is certain that the worst and most ruinous habits infecting the Indians occur among the common and lower orders but incidents are also reported among nobles and princes. Among the Spaniards you find many who lack Christian discipline and decent morals; they rub shoulders with negroes, mulattos and mestizos of various racial mixtures, and daily contact with them afflicts the Indian with vice, both in words and deeds, introducing him to impudence, shamelessness, malice, and the committal of misdeeds; he loses the fear of God and the regard and respect for his fellowmen.

The Indians, weak and sinners like all of us, used to have a sort of personal modesty, concealing their urges, either out of fear or shyness or for some other reason. It follows that when they felt like giving way to a weak impulse or commit a sin, they did confide in acquaintances, friends, or even in their parents. In our days those who have passed our schools still remain restrained, but many commit sins without fear and shame, even join and form gangs and plan and execute criminal actions. They brag of and are proud of misdeeds, claiming to have committed offences when they have not. They treat married women with foul language. What Indian would have dared in the pagan past to attack a strange woman and treat her as if she were his for the taking? Nobody would have done this, for everybody knew he would have to pay for it with his life, and that escape was impossible. As can be seen, they do this today without fear of retaliation. When in the past an Indian committed a theft, he was punished as a thief or pickpocket, but very few dared to steal. Since then they have imitated the Spaniards and other people and have developed into skilled robbers. Some operate on the highways; they have proper workshops for robbers. I cannot understand how their Christian conscience can allow people to tolerate thieves' kitchens to continue to operate in Indian towns, nor do I know how they can overlook their existence and other criminal activities during official inspections, for these activities deserve to be eradicated with fire and sword and their memory erased. Does anybody think they serve a good purpose? If so, why not introduce them into Spanish towns? The Indian bosses are the worst thieves, for they seize free men, and lock them up in Moorish fashion. Local Indians break into their houses and those of their neighbours when the captive's home remains unguarded.

Indians who have no contact with Spaniards or with servants of Spaniards have no doors on their houses and have no fear of losing anything; they even go to church without locking up. Today even doors, locks, and keys are no longer sufficient protection, for thieves climb low walls; it has led to a situation in which half the people stay at home for fear of finding an empty house on return from church; they miss mass. You could ask anybody, "Why do these Indian workers or servants of the Spaniards not attend mass? Why are they not in church?" And you will receive the reply: "They are not in church for they do what they like; as servants of the Spaniards they have a right to please themselves," and neither the king nor anyone else can stop them; they are out of control.

One of the worst damages inflicted by the Spaniards is the freedom to drink, for the natives are addicted to alcohol, which serves as an inducement and bait used by Spaniards to obtain control of native persons and property. And the easiest way for a Spaniard to deal with an Indian neighbour is to carry a cask of wine, when approaching him or his village. And when a dozen or fifteen Spaniards take up residence there, all or most of them become innkeepers. It would be impossible to list all the daily evils arising form this. After having too much to drink, friends kill one another, being quite unconscious of what they are doing. Many innocent wives are slain, for wine makes men wild. They beat their wives up with cudgels, and injuring wives is a daily occurrence. They sell their clothes to buy drink, and when nothing else is left to sell, they sell themselves. Married and marriageable women too frequent the taverns and sell themselves for wine. The chiefs and leading Indians also sell their land and houses, and when they have exhausted their capital they ask the Spaniards for a loan. And when nothing is left with which to repay the loan, they hire themselves out as workers. Others become idlers whom the country cannot support; they gamble and play the guitar, which they have learnt to strum from the Spaniards. Can you imagine that not only men but also women play cards and the guitar? Guitar players far exceed those who play cards in larger towns, and you hear more music than you like to hear.

Apart from this, the Spaniards arrange marriages for Indians. They may order the marriage of some Tom, Dick, or Harry with some woman of similar social class, if it offers an advantage to their staffing, personnel, and workforce, pointing out to the man and woman concerned what they might gain by marrying, then dragging them to the church and requesting the priest to unite them in wedlock; and that even when the couple do not know the Creed or even a few words of it, and all this without an enquiry into possible impediments. Because such unions do not originate from mutual affection, the participants soon separate, with each partner going his or her own way. You also often find that one or the other is already married in some other village.

Looking at the foul language now used by the Indians, we become convinced that they did not speak like that in their past when they were ignorant of swearing, cursing, and citing the devil; we believe that in the past they behaved more like our early Christians. Now all, and particularly women, have become addicted to foul language, disgraceful and a pain to listen to.

We can also observe a changed attitude of women concerning the upbringing of their small sons and daughters. In the olden days they taught their children honesty, humility, obedience, and respect, a training almost as strict and beneficial as that recommended for the religious novices. Children aged four or five behaved like people of fifty, almost like angels in heaven, and this to such an extent that when the friars first saw Indian chiefs take pulque they said in their conversation, "Surely these children should be the heads and magistrates in villages, for in their early years they possess the requisite brains and the maturity which the others may lose as a result of drink." This was the condition of native children in the past but this is no longer so now. Coming to our Spaniards: they have large families, and children can be found everywhere, in every hook, nook and corner, and they are up to a thousand mischiefs. They grow up, mixed up with Indian children, acquire rudeness, daring, and impudence in the pursuit not of salvation but hastening towards perdition.

Though the social evils I have listed are of grave consequence, I shall conclude with another one, which has been little discussed so far but which, in my poor opinion, should be investigated and put right, and this for the honour, respect, and reverence due to our Lord God. I refer to the sparse attendance of Spanish men and women, living in Indian locations, of the divine offices.

(The rest of the chapter enlarges on the purely Spanish theme.)

Chapter 35 : Sneezing - the result of acculturation?

When I first met the Indians, it was most exceptional to find one sneezing, and this filled me with surprise for a long time afterwards. The absence of sneezing was quite obviously due to their eating what nature prescribed to them as their substenance, to wit never more than two or three maize tortillas, prepared with some vegetable and chili, which latter we call in Spain "Indian pepper". As a result they did not develop cardinal humours requiring evacuation from the body. Today children on their mother's breast already sneeze, having inherited this from their parents who eat meat and the same viands as consumed by Spaniards, all of which cause a surfeit of fatty fluids. Now these natives sneeze as we do.

Chapter 36 : Epidemics and the work of the friars

Smallpox caused the first epidemic of a disease unknown in Mexico before the conquest. It was introduced by a negro on one of the ships of Captain Pánfilo de Narváez who in 1520 arrived to dislodge Cortés, but failed to do so. His men landed and infected the people in their villages, and thus spread the disease which left not a single corner of New Spain unaffected. In some provinces the entire population perished, and everywhere the casualty rate reached great heights. The cause of death from this disease was not known in the Indies and they had no cure for smallpox. The first friars who were destined to become the physicians of the Indians, both in a physical and a spiritual sense, had not yet arrived. Moreover the frequent hot baths which both the healthy and the sick took, inflamed their blood. There was death everywhere. It also lead to deaths from starvation, for those stricken with the illness could not look after others and provide them with food. In some regions all the occupants of a house died, burial became impossible, and homesteads turned into sepulchres. The survivors called the disease *Huey záhuatl* which means "the great leprosy", for the sick were covered with festering swellings from head to foot.

The second epidemic was like the first, imported from abroad eleven years after the first. This time it was measles, carried by a Spaniard and passed on to the Indians. Many died from it, though not as many as had died from smallpox, for time had taught them a lesson; they took precautions and listened to the advice not to take baths; they also took preventive medicaments. They called the sickness *Tepiton Záhuatl*, meaning "small leprosy", it being less pernicious. The New World did however pay us back, if we be permitted to use the word "pay", by carrying syphilis to Europe, an endemic disease of the New World, never before known in Europe.[48]

The third and most widespread epidemic struck in 1545, most likely a re-emergence of the two previous outbreaks. The symptoms were haemorrhages and high temperature. 150,000 persons died in Tlaxcala, 100,000 in Cholula and similar numbers in other cities.

(There follow details of epidemics in 1564 and 1576.)

Towards the end of the year 1595 and at the beginning of 1596, at the time when I finished this book, there came upon us another widespread epidemic, a combination of measles, mumps and typhoid fever, affecting practically everybody. Thanks to God's most benefic clemency and compassion the death-roll remained lower than in previous outbreaks. And this, I am convinced, was for three reasons: in the first place because our loving Heavenly Father arranged for the epidemic to strike after the completion of the harvest and the storing of the agricultural products; had it come earlier, very few of the Indians would have had a chance of survival. Secondly, as on all previous occasions of similar calamities and sickness, the friars looked after the sick and their souls, confessing them, administering holy communion and extreme unction, but on this occasion also giving physical support by providing them with food and, this time, with treatment and medicaments. With exemplary zeal the friars exerted themselves, causing admiration among the people. I intend to give you a description of the events in the city of Texcoco which lies half a league from the religious house where I was staying.

The father-superior of the house, Fray Juan Baptista, provided himself, at the beginning of the epidemic, which was to last two full months, with the medical supplies he reckoned he would require. When the Indians arrived for their confession, on foot or on stretchers and as best as sick people can manage, the superior had barbers in attendance who, after the confession, bled the visitors in the porter's lodge; there they would be made to rest for a while and those suffering from coughs were given syrup of cassia in lukewarm water. On some days they dispensed four large earthenware pots full of this syrup; some 300 patients might pass through on a very busy day, but usually not more than 200 or 250. Pregnant women, who could not be bled, had their swellings lanced on their back and were dosed with antidotal herbs, in Mexico called *Cohuane-nepilli*, taken with hot pulque; this usually cured them. Children had their legs lanced and were given the same mixture. They used to purge all patients with a singularly effective root, called *Matlalítzic*, superior to that of Michoacán, or another root called *Ytźic tlanoquiloni*. Others were given syrup of cassia, always in line with the treatment prescribed by the leading town physician and on his instructions. When they were handed purgatives and took them away, they were instructed how to use them. The most seriously sick patients received from Father Juan Baptista, the superior, quince jelly and other preserves which he had brought from Mexico City.[49]

You have to visualize what the porter's lodge and the convent patio looked like in those days: it was filled with a large number of patients, some being confessed, others bled, still others dosed with syrup; some were treated or just consoled. The very angels came to succour and strengthen us in this ministry! Consider also the effort required to cope with so many different medical problems, and that in addition to many of our brethren being sick themselves. The ones who remained immune even went out to visit sick Indians in the city and in distant places, all those who who were unable to come to the convent. They went in the company of barbers and carried purgatives and everything else required. They first confessed the sick and afterwards attended to their physical needs at their bedside. Those who developed diarrhoea were given the local remedies which cured them. The care, so diligently applied, was the second reason why fewer lives were endangered and fewer persons died than in previous outbreaks.

The third reason, and this is the honest truth, was that our Father of Compassion arranged for the arrival in New Spain, at this time, of a new viceroy, the most excellent and pious Don Gaspar de Fonseca y Zúñiga, Conde de Monterrey, who did much to keep the Indian population alive, by not permitting Indians to render personal services or work for Spaniards, unless they were paid for this. No previous viceroy had insisted on this, in the face of the Spaniards regarding it almost as their divine right to exact unpaid Indian labour.[50]

Chapter 44 :   Native languages: the general linguistic situation and the Franciscan contribution

The blessed doctors, Saints Jerome and Isidore, wrote special tracts in which they informed the faithful of the ecclesiastic authors of the early church. Following in their footsteps I felt that I should devote a special chapter to this theme, which would demonstrate how much we owe to the pioneers of the Church of New Spain, God's vineyard, who not content with clearing the ground, tilled and watered it with the sweat of brethren, and made it possible and easier for those who followed. They achieved this by employing the native language (language being the most essential element in the preaching of the Holy Gospel) and by their instruction in the Christian life. We owe those who composed or translated tracts into Náhuatl and other native languages an enormous debt, for like the blessed Apostles, they were inspired by the Holy Spirit. Their mastery of these languages is an example of devout application and human diligence; they became linguistic experts.

It started with some of the twelve first arrivals and among them Fray

Francisco Jiménez was the first to compose a Mexican vocabulary, while Fray Toribio Motolinia wrote a brief Christian catechism which at once appeared in print. Fray Juan de Ribas composed a catechism and sermons for every Sunday of the year, entitled "Flos Sanctorum" ("Flower of Saints"), short and precise, with questions and answers regarding the Christian life. Fray García de Cisneros also wrote sermons, and all these friars belonged to the first twelve Franciscans.

Fray Pedro de Gante, a lay brother, composed a long catechism which was also published. Fray Juan de San Francisco wrote a book of sermons, distinguished by its accomplished style, as well as some critical collections of the exemplary acts of saints, most suitable material for sermons to the Indians. Fray Alonso de Herrera wrote a book of Sunday sermons in Náhuatl, paying particular attention to the saints. Fray Alonso Rengel mastered Náhuatl and produced a book of sermons for the entire year. He also created a similar work in the Otomí language. Fray Andrés de Olmos possessed an exceptional gift for languages, for in Náhuatl he composed outstanding work, most probably the most comprehensive then available; but he also produced a vocabulary in Náhuatl, and vocabularies in the Totonac and Huástec languages. It is said that he was also conversant with the language of the Chichimecs.[51]

Fray Aranaldo de Bassacio, a Frenchman and an excellent theologian, wrote many lengthy sermons in exquisite Náhuatl and translated the Epistles and the Gospels, which were read throughout the year. Fray Juan de Gaona, a most learned man, became expert in Náhuatl and in that language composed some admirable tracts, which unfortunately are now lost; he also produced some dialogues or colloquies, the elegant style of which we can still enjoy, for they appeared in print; he also wrote a passion of our Redeemer.

Fray Bernardino de Sahagún composed sermons in the Mexican

language, covering the entire liturgical year, some long, some short, and also a gloss on the Sunday gospels and other tracts, all most polished. As a man who dug deep into the secrets and profundity of Náhuatl, he composed a Calepino,[52] consisting of twelve or thirteen volumes of high quality, which I am fortunate enough to have in my possession. Sahagún in this work describes the manner in which the Aztecs conversed on every imaginable subject, and enlarges on their morals, behaviour, religion, education, etc. The work, being so massive, was too large for a single man to translate. One of the viceroys took it out of his hands and asked some chroniclers to produce a translation of the passages concerning the Indians. The man accepted the proposal, but treated the translation with neglect, and all he published in the end, was a book of hymns. The Indians sang them when they danced. It was an edifying book, the text dealing with the life of the Saviour and his saints, designed to make the Indians forget their iniquitous customs of the pagan past. Fray Alonso de Escalona wrote many fine sermons, still appreciated today by all preachers; they were designed for Sunday and feast-day services. He also composed a tract about the Ten Commandments.

All of Fray Alonso de Molina's work has been published, including a Náhuatl vocabulary, a large and a smaller catechism, a translation of the Holy Sacraments and a Life of our Father St Francis. Apart from this, he translated the Gospels for the entire church year, as well as the prayers to Our Lady, though they were never pronounced in the profane language [i.e. only in Latin]. He translated many sermons to be addressed to the natives in order to widen their knowledge and enrich their Christian experience.

Fray Luis Rodríguez translated the Proverbs of Solomon most elegantly and also the four books of the *Contemptus Mundi*, though he omitted the last twenty chapters which were later to be translated by Fray Juan Baptista, who is the present superior of the monastery in Texcoco, where he has corrected all the books, expunging many errors which were due to the negligence of the copiers; they are now ready to be published. Fray Juan de Romanones wrote many stylish sermons and tracts and also translated sections of Holy Scripture. Fray Maturino Giberti, a Frenchman, published in the Tarascan language of Michoacán a book on Christian learning, containing everything a Christian needs for his salvation. Fray Francisco de Toral, Bishop of Yucatan, was the first person to understand and speak the language of Tecamacinco. He wrote a vocabulary and some instructional tracts. Fray Andrés de Castro, the "apostle" of the Matlatzinca[53] nation, wrote a grammar, vocabulary, catechism, and sermons in their idiom.

The saintly Fray Juan de Ayora, provincial of Michoacán, left, among other papers, a tract on the Holy Mass. Fray Juan Baptista de Lagunas, also a principal of Michoacán, writing in the Tarascan language, published tracts on Christian art and teaching. Fray Pedro de Palacios, an expert of the Otomí language, wrote a catechism and also a manual of instruction how to learn the language, later amplified by Fray Pedro Oroz, to whom we owe much gratitude for the massive work undertaken in both Otomí and Náhuatl, in which he composed many sermons which, pleasing God, have become most popular.

The Mexican language [Náhuatl] is the lingua franca in the provinces of New Spain, but in addition each province, and even some towns, have their own languages and the number of idioms is massive. However, interpreters are available everywhere, all speaking Náhuatl, which plays the part here that Latin plays in Europe. From my own knowledge I can state that Náhuatl is in no way inferior to Latin; I even feel it is more artistic in its composition and in the derivation of words, in metaphors, the meaning of which have been lost. Unfortunately its everyday use has led to increased corruption of the idiom. The Spaniards do not speak it; negroes and other foreign trash use our language. Even the Indians speak *castellano* and forget the language of their fathers and ancestors. Something not dissimilar is happening to our own Spanish, which is being corrupted by the intrusion of words our men have picked up during the conquest of the islands and words taken from Náhuatl.

To sum up: a conglomerate of languages, customs, and of persons of different natural origin has turned this country into a wild melting pot and this represents a major impediment to the spreading of the Christian faith among the new people. Would God change this!

BOOK V (PART I)

Franciscan brethren who died a natural death

Chapter 13 : The disappearance of the body of Fray Martín de Valencia

(The Valencia where this friar was born was not the great Mediterranean city but Valencia de Don Juan, a small place, situated half-way between the towns of León and Benavente. Mendieta devotes the first sixteen chapters of the Fifth Book to the brother, who was the leader of the group of twelve Franciscans, the first to arrive in New Spain in 1524. We have already dealt with the chapter (Bk. III, Ch. 12). He died on 31 August 1533. His successors ascribed to him almost saintly qualities as well as miracles and visions, but he has never been canonized.)

His saintly body remained incorrupt for more than 13 years. They opened his tomb on various occasions for the benefit of the friars of our own Order as well as those of St Dominic who wished to see the body, and the superiors of the monastery had similar wishes. But since 1567 the body has not been seen, though the tomb has been opened on several occasions. Was it God's wish for the body to disappear? Was the disappearance a reaction to an excess of curiosity or, better expressed, temptation, which led men to inter and disinter so many times a body which had the reputation of true sanctity? It may be that in response to the irreverence and temptation, Our Lord removed this sacred token and now keeps it safe, with only He himself in His Majesty knowing its place of concealment; perhaps in the fullness of time, certainly not in our days, it will be displayed once more, maybe even on the Day of Judgement and during the Resurrection of all that have been born into this world, when they assume their human form and present themselves before Christ's tribunal.

And I, Fray Gerónimo de Mendieta, the author of this book, confess that I too have been guilty of the same temptation and error, but not quite as much as others, for it was I who discovered the disappearance of the body! This came about in the following manner: In 1567 I accompanied the Provincial of the Province of the Holy Gospel [New Spain], then Fray Miguel Navarro. We arrived at the town of Tlamanalco, the site of the holy man's tomb. As I had gathered from reliable friars that the body of the saintly man was intact and without corruption and that a year, more or less, had passed since the sepulchre had last been visited, I persuaded the Provincial that we both should go and see the remains.

We took some Indians with us who raised the cover of the tomb with crowbars. The sepulchre had some depth, yet we did not find the body, nor the slightest trace of it, except some splinters and chips of wood, traces of the coffin in which he had been laid to rest. We started a searching inquiry among the leading villagers and among those who worked in the monastery, for without being noticed it would have been impossible to remove the saintly body, yet we found nothing at all. Nor did the friars have any idea. To this very day nothing has become known, and in 1580 an apostolic letter dealt with this matter, full of the gravest censure.

Chapter 18 : The Life of Fray Pedro de Gante

Fray Pedro de Gante was born in Flanders. In order to escape the temptations of the world and the pleasures of the flesh, with which the devil tempts and attracts young men at a time when their sap rises, he took the burden of Our Lord and the habit of our Father St Francis. Out of modesty he chose to remain a lay brother, which move showed his humility and deep-seated Christianity. He lived in the convent of Ghent when he heard the news, which spread like wildfire round the world, of Don Hernando Cortés's discovery and conquest of New Spain, on the mainland of America, and that Cortés had found the land inhabited by a large and numerous heathen population.

Impelled by the spirit of God and the need of salvation of souls, he joined the party of the superior Fray Juan de Tecto.[54]

Fray Pedro de Gante was an accomplished craftsman and well-versed in all trades required in a civilized country. It looks as if Our Lord sent him at the very start of the campaign for the conversion of the Indians, who were in need of just this kind of help and his guidance, not only in the spiritual sphere to save souls, but also in worldly tasks; in short, he was to open the eyes of the barbarians to spiritual concerns in accordance with the words of the apostle: "*Panis quod animale, deinde quod spirituale*" [Corinthians, 15:46. "Howbeit that was not which is spiritual but that which is natural and afterward that which is spiritual"]. He was the first one in New Spain to teach natives to read, write, sing, and play musical instruments. In Texcoco, very early on, he taught the sons of the princes and that before the arrival of the twelve. Later he did the same in Mexico City, where he lived for the rest of his life, with the exception of a short spell of duty in Tlaxcala. He was instrumental in the building of the solemn and sumptuous chapel of San José behind the modest and small church, the first, of St Francis, where the Indians assembled to hear the word of God and watch the performance of the divine office; they listened to the Christian message on Sundays and feast-days and received the holy sacraments. He also built a school for boys, where initially he taught the sons of princes and chiefs from all over New Spain, but which today is reserved for children of Mexico City.

Adjoining the school he arranged other rooms and houses to be taken over for lessons in painting; here the Indians created images and retables for churches all over New Spain. Others were instructed in masonry, carpentry, tailoring, smithery, and other mechanical trades, to enable them to get acquainted with these crafts and practise them. Adjoining the school, Fray Pedro had a cell, whither he could withdraw each day or now and then. There he spent time in prayer, reading and doing spiritual exercises. He then returned to his school to see what his pupils did. It was his principal concern to ensure that all his students left well instructed, both in Christian knowledge and in reading, writing, and singing, all subjects they studied. And when they grew up, he expected them to spread the faith and, regularly on Sundays and feast-days, to attend mass and listen to God's word.

He interviewed those who intended to get married, and prepared those who were to receive the holy sacrament of the Eucharist. He preached when no priest was available to do so, and in the native language, which he knew very well, though having been born a stutterer; in spite of this his brethren could understand him very well, both in Spanish and in Náhuatl. It bordered on a miracle that the natives understood him so well although he was not one of theirs.

He composed a catechism and had it published in a large edition. He founded confraternities, all of which have endured. He continuously added to the external embellishment of divine worship, providing singers as well as artisans, especially for services held in the Chapel of San José; he supplied the frames to be carried in processions, which as a result of his industry became more plentiful than in other Christian cities.

He built many churches in the city itself and in its environs. The fifty years he lived there he spent in setting the most splendid example of a pure person, always impressing with his apostolic honesty, never working for anything but the glory and honour of God and the edification of souls, a countless number of which he gained for Christ. Because of this he was much loved; also for the purity of his life. Although remaining a lay brother, he preached to and confessed the Indians like other great servants of God and prelates of his Order. They accepted and recognized him as a priest. They came to him with all their daily worries, troubles, and concerns. The good order among the natives of the entire city of Mexico and its vicinity depended on him in all spiritual and church matters. So much so, that the second archbishop, Fray Alonso de Montúfar, a Dominican, used to say: "It is not I who am archbishop of Mexico, but Fray Pedro, a Franciscan lay-brother." It is true that he could easily have been archbishop, had he agreed to enter the priesthood, for the Emperor Charles V, of glorious memory, a compatriot of his, was fully informed of his person and life and thought much of him. They say that he invited him to become archbishop of Mexico.

He loved the native Indians dearly, and in order to ensure the instruction of the greatest possible number, he wrote letters to Flemish brethren of his own nation, exhorting them to come to the New World to cultivate the Lord's vineyard then so short of workers. In return, the natives loved this servant of God greatly, particularly those in Mexico City. This became evident when Fray Pedro returned from Tlaxcala where he had been ordered to stay awhile. They came out to receive him in a fleet of handsome canoes on the Lake of Texcoco, arranging a special display for him in the shape of a naval skirmish, and all expressed their pleasure at his return.

An Indian woman used to express her devotion by making habits for the brethren, and in this pursuit she met Fray Melchior de Benavente, who at that time was in charge of the Indians in the Chapel of San José. She said to him: "Padre, I would like to make six habits for you friars", and she named them, including Fray Pedro who was already dead. Fray Melchior de Benavente replied: "My daughter, did you not know that Fray Pedro de Gante has quitted this life and has died?" She replied: "I give a habit to Fray Pedro as an offering; give it to whom you like." Such was the love the natives had for this servant of God even after his passing away.

Fray Pedro de Gante laboured much in this vineyard of Christ, particularly early on, smashing idols and destroying their temples. He built more than one hundred churches where today they invoke the name of the true God. The devil tempted him to return to Flanders and to abandon his magnificent enterprise, but with God's help he defeated the tempter, cut the ties that had bound him and served God; he actually discloses this in a letter written to his parents in Flanders.

He was a man of the utmost humility; he demonstrated this by declining to accept and to act on three special licences, authorizing his elevation to the priesthood, the first issued by Pope Paul III, the second by Fray Vicente Luniel, general of the Order, at the general chapter in Rome, who felt that a man of his stature should not remain a lay brother. The third was issued by the Apostolic Nuncio at the court of the Emperor Charles V, probably at the time when the Emperor wanted to appoint him archbishop, a fact we have mentioned earlier on. But this servant of Christ spurned vanity like dirt. His sole ambition was to persist in his original vocation in the spirit which had led him to a monastic life.

He died in 1572. His death led to a public expression of painful grief. An enormous crowd attended his funeral, abundant tears were shed by all who felt they had lost a true father. Solemn obsequies were arranged everywhere, particularly in each confraternity, each town and village of the vicinity, and huge offerings were made. In addition, each year the anniversary of his death was celebrated, and the natives supplied the Monastery of San Francico in Mexico with food and other necessities.

The Indians asked the heads of the Franciscan Order to inter the body in the Chapel of San José. They agreed, and until now his sepulchre is the object of much veneration. The sepulchre is crowned by a painting, made from life. Portraits of him can also be seen in the principal towns of New Spain, together with those of the twelve founders of the Province of the Holy Gospel [New Spain].

Chapter 29 : The death of Fray Juan de Zumárraga, First Archbishop of Mexico

(Fray Juan de Zumárraga (c.1470-1548), a devout and learned man, who from the moment of his arrival in New Spain until his death endeavoured to protect the natives from the greed and oppression of the *conquistadores* and the colonists, at one time even facing personal danger from the members of the Audiencia. It was Torquemada (Vol. I, Bk. 3) who first stated that the friars burnt also other objects of great importance for the knowledge of facts connected with New Spain, to wit sheets of native "books", "covered with figures and characters representing fictitious and natural animals - all encapsulating superstitions and pagan practices; and they burnt as many as they could lay hands on". Clavigero supported this view, which was to find its fiercest expression in Prescott (Bk. I, Ch. 4): "The first archbishop of Mexico, Don Juan de Zumárraga, a name that should be as immortal as that of Omar, collected these paintings from every quarter, especially from Texcoco, the most cultured capital of Anáhuac and the great depository of the national archives. He caused them to be piled up in a mountain heap, as it is called by Spaniards writers themselves, and in the market-place of Tlatelolco he reduced them all to ashes. We contemplate this with indignation as one of the cruelties inflicted by the early conquerors." Prescott's indictment has been infectuous, and many historians repeat the accusation, adding curses of their own; for instance Walter Krickeberg (*Altmexikanische Kulturen*, Berlin, 1975) who speaks of Zumárraga's *Zerstoerungswut* ("destructive mania") or Jacques Soustelle (*Daily life of the Aztecs*) who speaks of "the fanatical hands of Zumárraga". A saner view is taken by J. H. Parry, op. cit. (pp. 161-2). For a good summary we recommend Lesley Bird Simpson, *Many Mexicos*, (Berkeley, 1967) pp. 43-4, footnote 1.

At dinnertime they offered him a little wine, but however much they pressed him and tried to persuade him, they failed to make him drink, though his age and fatigue and state of health made some refreshment vital. In this manner he acted, because he knew that the friars in this convent [the Dominicans of Tepetlauztoc] suffered from a shortage of drinks. And he did not regard himself more important than they were. He spent four days there, discussing with them whether to accept or reject the offer of the archiepiscopal dignity. He also confirmed 14,500 Indians, an enormous effort for a man so advanced in years. This is a fact, confirmed by the records.

On the Thursday after Easter, the bladder complaint from which he suffered developed with painful intensity and compelled him to return to the city, accompanied by his friend, Fray Domingo de Betanzos, who never left his side and looked after him until he expired in his very arms, something Fray Juan had hoped for. An hour before his death he said to the friars who surrounded him: "My brethren, there is a great difference between a man in *articulo mortis* and one just talking about it." With the utmost devotion he received the sacraments of the Eucharist and Extreme Unction. He surrendered his soul to the Creator with the words: "*In manus tuas, Domine, commendo spiritum meum*" ["Into Your hand, Oh Lord I surrender my soul"]. This happened on the Sunday after Corpus Christi, at nine in the morning, in the year 1548. He died in full possession of his senses, undisturbed, aged more than eighty years. In accordance with his instructions, he was interred with his brethren in the monastery of San Francisco, but since he had been the first prelate of the church of New Spain, they buried him in the porch of the sanctuary, adjoining the high altar, on the gospel side, the most prominent location of all.

Miraculously the news of his death spread all over New Spain the very day it occurred and caused general mourning in all towns and villages. A great many people visited his tomb, and so many tears were shed by the friars and the people that they found it difficult to lay him to rest. No prelate had ever before been mourned with such intense feelings of grief. The viceroy and the judges of the *Audiencia* attended the obsequies, dressed in long black gowns, unable to suppress their sobbing. The mourning and weeping of the ordinary people too was overwhelming, giving the impression that the Day of Judgement had arrived. They say that his body remained uncorrupt, and it is certain that after his death, Our Lord has performed some miracles for His servant.

The most authentic miracle refers to the fact that some years before his death he had prohibited some indecent dances and representations, performed in connection with the general procession at the Feast of Corpus Christi. This, in his fair judgement, required a dignified and reverential performance. In order to ensure the observation of this reforming measure, once and for all, he published, in conjunction with a tract by Dionisio Cartujano, a catechism expressing the view that processions should always be performed with dignity and reverential comportment. After his death and while the archiepiscopal seat was still vacant, this servant of God appeared to some members of the chapter who had been responsible for the dances in the past. As they were getting ready, on the day of the holy feast, it began to rain cats and dogs in the morning, and this made it impossible to hold a street procession. Seeing this, the chapter realised that on the suggestion of this saintly man, heaven had intervened to prevent them from breaking Zumárraga's rule. They decided that in future all performances and dances be removed from the festivities, and this rule was observed during the six years the see remained vacant.[55]

Chapter 38 : The labours of Fray Juan de San Francisco

(In Chapter 37 Mendieta relates that this friar has studied in Salamanca, there entered the Franciscan Order and had arrived in New Spain in 1529.)

It was in Tehuacán, a major city, that Fray Juan found his hands full in his effort to teach and convert. This place had previously been particularly dedicated to the religion and service of the false gods; its very name seems to mean "site of the gods", and it harboured a correspondingly large number of idols. Our servant of God collected as many as possible with the intention of staging, on a certain date, a solemn sacrifice to His Divine Majesty, by publicly destroying and burning these abominations. For this purpose he called the elders and chiefs together, and once they were assembled, he told them that it pleased Our Lord to see all the Indians of the region gather in this capital of the province on the day of the Apostles St Peter and St Paul [29 June], for he had many things to tell them. They should order their people to come, and this without fail and exception.

The chiefs did what the servant of God had ordered them to do, and when on the appointed day all were gathered, he preached a sermon in which he exposed the deceit and blindness into which the enemy of the human race had plunged them and their ancestors by inducing them to worship their ugly statues and offering them their blood and that of their children. This had been an offence and insult to the true God, who had created man in his image and likeness for the purpose of receiving his sacrifices and praises. When he had finished his sermon he commanded his loyal young men, whom he had taught the faith, to break those idols into pieces, which he had previously already lined up for this purpose. They did this at once, leaving not a single idol intact. With his own hands Fray Juan broke the principal figure into pieces, pronouncing the words of the psalmist: "*Similacra gentium, argentum et aurum* etc". ("The idols are silver and gold, the work of men's hands. They have mouths but speak not, they have eyes but see not, they have ears but hear not, they have noses but smell not." (Psalm 113, Pt. II, 2)) And he cut off the hands and feet of the idol, leaving only the trunk while pronouncing the words of the psalm. It left the mass of the infidels present at the spectacle in a state of amazement, but no one dared contradict him, who was there all on his own, supported only by some young men he had taught, the sons of the very unbelievers. Of course, he had on his side reason and faith and they just could not but comprehend that there existed one omnipotent God, invisible, and that those statues and effigies could not possibly be gods but were nothing but abominable and horrible objects.

Yet the accursed devil, the inventor of all evil, on this very day appeared to an Indian heathen, a native of Tehuacán, whose occupation demanded him to visit places at distances of twenty leagues and who, because of this, had not attended the meeting. The devil appeared to him in the shape of the very idol which, with his own hands, the friar had broken to pieces and fatally damaged. Satan said to the man, "Look what this Christian priest has done to me in Tehuacán." As a faithful pagan he should go at once to avenge this insult. The Indian said he would gladly do this, but that he was afraid of the chiefs and the people who took great care to protect the priest. The devil replied he should take a heavy cudgel, he should not be afraid, being after all a brave man, and that he, the devil, would help him. He should enter the monastery, hide in the very place where the priest usually stayed, and he should then seize and kill him. He could, thereafter, leave without being seen by anybody, and not a soul would ever know he had killed the priest.

The Indian went on his way to do what the devil had ordered, and he hid in the place indicated to him. As the blessed padre entered, this servant of the devil gave him a blow with his cudgel, expecting to have killed him, there and then; but Our Lord preserved him for greater causes; the assassin missed his mark and the cudgel slipped over Fray Juan's shoulders without doing him harm. In this situation Fray Juan shouted, his companions arrived and the Indian failed to escape. When he asked the Indian why he had wanted to kill him, he told in so many words that Satan had persuaded him to do so and in the manner we have described. The Indian, seeing his error, adopted the Christian faith and received baptism.

This apostolic man also converted countless natives, including the chief priest of the city of Tehuacán. When he was in Mexico, this Indian fell seriously ill. The devil appeared to him in the persons of his parents, saying that they dwelt in a most delightful region, enjoying untold comfort, and he should come and join them. They even took hold of him, taking him to a grove and asking him to hang himself. Persuaded by the demons to do so he was getting ready, when a friar appeared to him, in the shape of Fray Juan de San Francisco, who, at that time, as we have stated, resided in Mexico City; the friar reproached him for having forgotten so quickly all he had taught him. Why had he put his trust in demons, his enemies, who had adopted the appearance of his parents? The Indian now called on God, and the demons vanished and left him alone. This Indian was convinced that Friar Juan had appeared to him and when he left the city, he fell on his knees before the friar, asking his forgiveness for his errors and thanking him for having saved him from the very hell. When the saintly man learnt how Our Lord had saved the native from the devil's clutches, he gave thanks for His mercy and for having rescued this poor Indian. He exhorted the man from now on to follow the commands of Jesus Christ and never again to give credit to the lies and tricks of demons.

Chapter 39 : The story of Fray Juan de San Francisco, continued

A pious woman brought him a dead boy of hers, asking him most fervently to give him his blessing. The holy man blessed the dead child, and at once he rose in perfect health. The brethren wished to celebrate and acknowledge this extraordinary event, but he excused himself, saying that it had been through the mother's great faith that the boy had regained his life.

In this same monastery of Tehuacán, Fray Juan found himself one day in his cell in prayer when St Francis and St Claire appeared to him and spoke to him in the most friendly manner. Among other things, they said: "These Indians have what you yourself have vowed to preserve, poverty, obedience, and humility."

His life was full of miracles, and it is somewhat difficult to give a summary of them. Being unable to recite them and not wishing to become tedious, we shall now cease to speak of his life and deal with his happy death, a model and an example bearing witness to this man's quality. He was superior of the convent of Cuernavaca when a year before his death he informed Fray Rodrigo de Bienvenida, his chaplain, of the date, saying that he had to die before the next chapter would be held. Two months before the opening of the chapter he fell ill and Fray Rodrigo nursed him. Fray Juan said to him: "My brother, do not make a fuss over my health, for Fray Antonio de Ciudad Rodrigo has said 'what has to come, will come'." This last-named brother, one of the twelve early Franciscans, had by then been dead for more than two years. He had appeared to Fray Juan the previous night and told him to get ready, for his illness was terminal. He also told him many other things which he passed on to Fray Rodrigo, in particular that God was greatly upset by the lack of justice in New Spain. This actually happened almost forty days before his glorious death. What else he heard or knew, we cannot say, for he dealt with God's concerns.

He left for Mexico City, taking leave of all, for he knew he would never see them again. On arrival he received, with the utmost devotion, the holy sacraments, and when given extreme unction his eyes were trained upon the crucifix which his hands clasped. He completed his life hereunder, surrendering his soul to the Creator, reciting the words the Saviour of the World had pronounced on the Cross: "*In manus tuas, Dominem, commendo spiritum meum*" ("Into Thy hands, Oh Lord, I commend my spirit") (St Luke, 23, 46). He died at eleven o'clock, one Friday in the year 1556.

That day, about midnight, this holy man appeared to a pious Spanish lady in Cuernavaca, whose confessor he had been in his lifetime, and he told her that he had spent twelve hours in purgatory and that he was already on the way to glory. A few days later he also appeared to his close friend Fray Rodrigo who saw him quite unexpectedly next to himself, lying in his bed and filling the cell with a resplendant light, seizing his arm and saying he should lead a good life and serve God. Then he vanished. This Fray Rodrigo de Bienvenida was also a man of great holiness, and he vouchsafed for this incident on several occasions, and also confirmed it to me in writing, describing how he had seen the good Fray Juan in his vision, clad in his habit and spreading a light like that of the Sun. It is after all nothing unusual nor an expression of exaggerated admiration to say that some great servants of God and the Saints have undergone the trials of purgatory and there felt the need for some support. We read in the histories of the Church of men of great sanctity having undergone the tests of purgatory, spending sometime there, and this has not prevented them from performing miracles. St Severin, Bishop of Cologne, of whom Peter Damian writes, performed miracles while lodging in purgatory. Of the Deacan Pascasius, St Gregory says in his *Morales* that he was so holy that when they carried his body to the grave, a person, possessed, approached the bier, seizing his dalmatica, and that cured him at once. Later this Pascasius appeared to St Germanus, Bishop of Capua, and he told him that he had done penance, for in a certain schismatic dispute he had supported Lorenzo against Pope Symachus, when afterwards this Lorenzo had been cast off and sentenced.

(The remaining thirteen chapters deal with an impressive number of brethren. Because the stories are very similar, we have not translated them.)

BOOK V (PART II)
Franciscan Martyrs

Chapter 1 : The martyrdom of Fray Juan Calero

I maintain that Fray Juan Calero was the first of the early missionaries to suffer martyrdom in this land. I realize that of the ranks of the newly converted a boy named Cristóbal and some other Tlaxcaltecas had been martyred, as I have related in Chapters 25 and 27 of my Book III. Others regard a French friar, Fray Bernardo Cossin, as an earlier sufferer, but I say they are wrong, for they have not been acquainted with what Fray Toribio Motolinia had already written, and he can be absolutely relied upon to relate what happened in his day. With words of spiritual splendour he has added to his description of the martyrdom of Fray Juan Calero the following words: "I am praising God for two reasons. Firstly that he chose for his first martyr in the New World a member of the Order of the Friars Minor and a lay brother when so many others and many old priests fervently desired to die for Jesus Christ; for that purpose they had crossed the ocean and had lived among the heathens of the New World. But God chose this humble lay brother to confer on him the crown of martyrdom. The second reason for my giving thanks to God is that the first martyr was a son of a new church, who had taken the habit in this new Province of the Holy Gospel [New Spain], thirteen years before suffering a martyr's death. It confirms my conviction that it was God's design to confer the greatest mercy upon this new bride."[56]

These are the very words of Fray Toribio who evidently was convinced that the death of Fray Juan Calero preceded that of Fray Bernardo Cossin. Motolinia, when referring to a "first martyr", speaks of brethren who had come from Europe to these parts and not of martyrs in general. He became an eyewitness of the martyrdom of young Cristóbal years earlier when residing in the convent of Tlaxcala.[57]

In order to understand the circumstances which lead to the death of Fray Juan Calero, and that of his superior which followed, we have to know that in 1539 they founded a Franciscan convent in a place called Ezatlán in the province of New Galicia or Jalisco.[58] Father Antonio de Cuëllar was the first superior, who had taken the habit in the Monastery of San Francisco in Salamanca. He laboured ceaselessly to preach and to teach and attract the Indians of those parts, whom they call Chichimecs, to our holy faith, people who had never before heard of our God. Within the space of one year and a half he brought a great many villages to the obedience of our Holy Mother Church and the Catholic faith, baptizing many children as well as some adults who were ready to be converted. And some, who lived scattered in the mountains or in canyons, he brought together in *reducciones* or proper settlements in communities with the appropriate communal structure and regulations which we have in Spain.

At that time a chapter of the Order was held in the city of Mexico, in accordance with the regulations, and Fray Antonio de Cuëllar handed his duties as superior to another of his friars, who was to be assisted by a lay brother Fray Juan Calero, who, it appears, knew the Indian language and who had been a great help to the superior.

During the superior's absence in the year 1541, some Indians of the province of Jalisco staged a rising, calling themselves Caxacanes, abandoning their villages and abrogating the Christian faith. The rebellion started in the highlands of Tequila and from there spread to a village within the religious domain of Ezatlán, from which the natives had received the Christian faith.[59]

The superior was ignorant of the native language. Fray Juan, who had taught the rebellious natives, took the defection from the faith by those whom he had converted very badly; he had not placed them into settlements to find them eventually killed or made permanent slaves by the Spaniards. Impelled by his zeal for the salvation of the barbarians and out of feelings of Christian charity, he asked his superior for permission to enter the hill country to persuade the rebels to return to their villages. The priest, the acting superior, showed himself favourably inclined. He regarded the step suggested by Fray Juan as merciful and godly and not only encouraged him, but even commanded him to proceed. Fray Juan confessed and took communion, and commending himself, with the utmost devotion, to the Lord, in a sacred mood he took the path leading to the mountains then occupied by the rebels.

He reached Tequila [North-West of Guadalajara] where he addressed the natives in his usual manner, with great sympathy, and he reasoned with them on spiritual and devotional grounds, trying to persuade them not to abandon the faith they had embraced; they should save their souls. They should not be led astray by Satan, who wanted them to join him and take them to the eternity of hellfire. They should return to their villages where the friars, their spiritual fathers, who loved them like children, had settled them. He himself promised he would secure a pardon for any errors committed, even an amnesty for those who had slain Spaniards and those who had erected idols and invoked demons.

The Chichimecs who listened to his speech knew that Friar Juan was a person of unblemished character and that he loved them. They listened in silence, without interrupting him. They then replied that he should return to his monastery; they knew what was good for them and what action they had to take.

Seeing their determination and the impossibility of persuading them to come back with him, Fray Juan began to retrace his steps and return to his convent. It was now that other barbarians arrived who had not heard his address. They knew why this servant of God had come, and among them were also those responsible for the murder of Spaniards and other crimes; all these were inspired by Satan. They regarded it as an impudent affront on the part of the friar to have come to preach the faith of Christ and to attempt to deprive them of their ancient idolatry. So they decided to kill him, and for this purpose they followed him. Some say that an Indian woman egged them on and inflamed their minds against this servant of God, acting like another Jezebel inviting King Achab to kill the innocent Naboth, or like Herodias inciting King Herod against St John the Baptist (III Kings 21; Mark VI). She said they could not bear the name of "men" unless they killed that friar who had come to tell lies. In any case, the barbarians followed that gentle sheep with their bows and arrows, war-clubs, and hefty poles with reinforced points which they used as swords and or lances.

When the holy martyr saw them arrive in this hostile manner, he knew they had come to kill him. He fell on his knees, giving thanks to God for the great blessing of allowing him to die a martyr's death and for having allowed him to proclaim the holy faith. The barbarians discharged their arrows, and pierced by missiles, he fell to the ground, proclaiming the name of God in front of the unbelievers. Not satisfied with their handiwork, they smashed his mouth and teeth with their warclubs, exclaiming: "You will no longer preach about celestial things or hell; we have no need for your sermons!" They also gave him blows on the head. Blood was flowing from many parts of his body, and when they saw he was not quite dead, they finished him off, by stoning him.

It thus happened that this blessed martyr suffered the torments of the glorious Saints Stephen, Sebastian, Appolonia, and also of St Thomas of Canterbury, whose skull the murderers cracked.[60]

Friar Juan Calero had been accompanied by four Indian Christians, servants of the church, two of them young acolytes and the other two adults. Of the last-named one, Francisco, escaped and told those in Ezatlán what had happened. The other three did not wish to flee, but preferred to die with their master. In tears, they embraced each other, and in this very embrace the infidel barbarians killed them. We can be sure that their souls joined that of the saintly martyr in heaven.

They assumed in Ezatlán that the savages would carry the corpse off to eat it or to offer it to their idols, for this had been their habit. They therefore refrained from pursuing them. At the end of a period of five days they heard that the bodies were still lying on the ground. It was then that a Spanish Captain, Diego López de Zúñiga, with some of his men, set out. He found the body of the blessed Fray Juan fresh and uncorrupted, with even his blood as fresh as it had been before he was assailed. By contrast the bodies of his Indian companions had been eaten by foxes, wolves, or some other animals or carnivorous birds, native in this land and called turkey buzzards. When they espy a corpse lying on the ground, sometime at a great distance, they discover it with their extraordinary sense of smell, arrive and devour it. It is surely a miracle that the body of this saintly man remained intact for five long days, incorrupt and sweet-smelling, and this in the heat of the summer, for he died on 10 June 1541, on the first day of Whitsun.

They took his body to Ezatlán. The resident superior dressed it in a new habit, for the original one had taken by the savages as a beastly triumphal token. When they buried him, the Spaniards present were surprised by the fragrance which one, who had been dead so long, spread. They interred him with great devotion and solemnity and in an odour of sanctity.[61]

Chapter 4 : The martyrdom of Fray Bernardo Cossin, of Fray Juan de Tapia and some others

Having proved satisfactorily that Fray Bernardo Cossin was not the first friar dying at the hands of the Chichimecs, we have to place Fray Juan de Padilla [mentioned in Ch. 3] into second place and his superior in the third, for all their deaths occurred at the same time. We cannot be certain of the date of Fray Bernardo's demise.

We know that he was of French origin, a hard worker for the salvation of souls, anxious to lead the Indians to a knowledge of the true Creator, and that his fervour impelled him to enter the land of the Indian barbarians, the Chichimecs, advancing as far as the mountain range we Spaniards call Nueva Vizcaya, beyond the mines of Zacatecas. He was accompanied by some friendly Indians and came in peace. Crossing the mountain range was laborious and dangerous, but he continued with his work of evangelization. He happened to come across some Indian savages who, aiming their bows at him, fired arrows to kill him, but these arrows turned round against those who discharged them and the Indians, in utter confusion, took to their heels. He advanced as far as the valley of Guadiana, and there this Christian vanguard rested. He gave sermons to the natives. While he was engaged in this holy work, a few days later some ungrateful and inhuman savages killed him, incited, of course, by Satan, who (with divine licence) did this to release them from the true faith. And yet, in the course of time, many of them accepted Christianity and received baptism.

In 1555 Chichimec savages cruelly killed two Franciscan friars, but though I was at that time already resident in New Spain and had learnt the native language, I could not ascertain their names, and those who knew them have all died. All I know is that one was an old priest and the other a younger man.

In 1556 Fray Juan de Tapia entered the valley of Guadiana, moving beyond the mines of Zacatecas. He had taken his habit in the province of La

Concepción; he now preached the Gospel and carried the word of God to the barbaric dwellers of those parts. In a very short time he baptised 10,000 Indians, and after this memorable feat he returned to the city of Guadalajara, the episcopal seat of New Galicia, where he attended a meeting of the chapter and gave an account of his work in the wilderness to the bishop. He had brought with him some of the converted Chichimecs to demonstrate to the prelate the necessity of Christian teaching. Moved by this the bishop authorized him to return to the country of the savages and to continue there the work of converting souls. Armed with this licence the friar returned to his labours of charity, but on the road, four leagues from Zacatecas, Indians, called Guachichiles, shot him with arrows. The servant of God sank to his knees, holding his crucifix in his hands, and expired. As a religious man he had led a most laudable life, pursuing the conversion of infidels with exemplary fervour and spending his entire life in this holy enterprise. He was assisted by an Indian lay person, called Lucas. Fray Juan's body was taken to the monastery in Zacatecas in the Province of the Holy Gospel [New Spain].[62]

NOTES

[1] In the subsequent Treaty of Tordesillas (7 June 1494), Spain and Portugal agreed to have the demarcation line at 270 leagues to the west. This gave the Portuguese the right to occupy Brazil.

[2] Father Bernardo Buil (Boil, Boyl, Buyl), born in 1445, a native of Tarragona. Before making his profession in the Monastery of Montserrat he had been a mariner. He stood in high regard with King Ferdinand who, even after the man's ordination in 1481, employed him on confidential and diplomatic missions.

[3] Columbus's second voyage began in Cadiz on 25 September 1493, with some seventeen ships, 1,200 expeditionaries and 700 soldiers.

[4] Father Buil returned to Spain and there denounced, in the gravest manner, Columbus's administration, accusing him, among other things, of abuse of his authority. He later became abbot of San Miguel de Cuxa in Roussillon, and there he died in 1520. He is mentioned by Las Casas (*Historia*, Bk. I, Ch. 81), who confirms his ineffectiveness in Española (see also Chs. 42, 92, 100 and 109). Samuel Eliot Morison, the distinguished modern biographer of Columbus, has this to say: "Buil was a bad egg indeed. He and the other friars under his orders had done absolutely nothing to convert and instruct the docile Tainos" (p. 484). See also Torquemada, Vol. III, Bk. 18, Ch. 6.

[5] *Cazabe* = cassava bread. A concise description of the processes involved and the yuca or manioc plant, is given in Oviedo's *Sumario* (Ch. V). Morison: "The women sold them a quantity of cassava roots and taught them how to make cassava bread by rasping the roots of the yuca or manioc on a wooden grater with flints imbedded in its surface, leaching out the hydrocygenic acid, which the Caribs used to make poison for their arrows, kneading the flour into a dough, patting it into thin cakes and baking it over the fire on a griddle made of ironware . . . It retains its flavour and freshness for a long time." Oviedo regarded it as superior to ship's biscuits and certainly to any other type of cornbread. (Morison, p. 499)

[6] The *blanca* was an ancient Castilian copper coin of varying value. The *castellano* or *peso de oro* was worth about 475 *maravedíes* and weighed 0.16 oz. or 4.55 g.

[7] This chapter tallies with Las Casas's strictures. The destruction of the islanders, not only by means of inhuman treatment but also through epidemics, was already "old history" when Mendieta put his pen to paper. See Las Casas, *Brevísima Relación* (p. 81); also his *Historia* (Bk. II, Ch. 42); Motolinia (Trat. I, Ch. 3); Gómara, *Historia* (Ch. 33); and Oviedo, in particular his *Historia General*, for a detailed survey of Española and the early colonial years, for he arrived early and ended his life as the commandant of the fortress of Santo Domingo (esp. Bk. I, pp. 75-140 and 143-52).

[8] Fray Andrés de Olmos's work is unfortunately lost. His life and work are described by Mendieta in Bk. V (1), Chs. 33-35.

[9] This is just one of the many creation myths, all of which are distinguished by irrational confusion. Compare with Sahagún, Bk. III, Chs. 1 ff.; Durán, Vol. I, Chs. 1-23 (who does not discuss the origins, but in Vol. II, Ch. 2 states that the México-Aztecs emerged from the Seven Caves in the year AD 820); Francisco Hernández, Bk. III, Ch. r; Torquemada, Vol. I, Bk. 1, Chs. 11-12 and Vol. II, Bk. 6, Ch. 7. Also Miguel León-Portilla, *Aztec Thought and Culture*, pp. 25 ff.

[10] Although we have used the word "pyramidal structure" and are dealing with a step-pyramid, the author does not use this term at all. Some *teocalli* have survived, and they can be studied in Teotihuacán, Tenayuca and in Yucatan. Mendieta's description lacks precision; he evidently has never seen a *teocalli*, the reason being that all visible traces had been expunged by the Spaniards. The great temple pyramids surviving owe their rescue to the fact that most of them had been covered with earth and looked like natural eminences. The Mexican *teocalli* has nothing in common with the Egyptian pyramid but is closely related to the Mesopotamian Ziggurat. For the architectural aspects, see George Kubler, *The Art and Architecture of Ancient America*, or Pal Keleman, *Medieval American Art*; for the lay-out of cities, Jorge E. Hardoy, *Pre-Columbian Cities*.

[11] Quetzalcóatl remains something of a mystery, for he appears in a variety of roles: (a) as a god, worshipped long before the arrival of the Aztecs in the Valley of Mexico and, perhaps only reluctantly included in their host of deities, for originally he refused human sacrifices, loving butterflies and flowers. In Cholula he demanded human blood; (b) as a culture hero, resembling the Andean Viracocha, a white-faced, bearded apostle, bringing true religion and civilization to a scarcely human race; spurned and rejected he leaves, promising to return; (c) as a king of the Toltecs. Forced to flee from his capital Tula, a victim of his enemy Tezcatlipoca; (d) the historic conqueror of Yucatan under the Maya name of Kukulkán; (e) overall a messianic saviour who will fulfil his promise and return from the east. Modern interpreters: León-Portilla, *Aztec Thought and Culture*; Laure de Séjourné, *La pensée des anciens Mexicains* (Paris, 1982). Some earlier authors even identified the man with the Apostle St Thomas.

[12] The volcano referred to is Popocatépetl (popoca = smoke; tépetl = mountain), 17, 794 feet above sealevel.

[13] The artificial mound created for the ancient *teocalli* still exists in Cholula, but it is now crowned by a magnificent church, consecrated to Nuestra Señora de Remedios.

[14] References to the continued role played by Satan, who is usually identified with a pagan god, occur in practically all the writings. The Fiend is shown to resent his expulsion and loss of control. See: Motolinia, Trat. 2, Ch. 8; Sahagún, Bk. V, for comments on the role of owls; also ibid., Chs. 4 and 11-13; Torquemada, Vol. I, Bk. 1, Ch. 14, and Vol. II, Bk. 6, Ch. 47; for ghosts in detail, ibid., Bk. 14, Ch. 22.

[15] Giants are frequently mentioned in colonial literature. Reports were invariably based on fossil remains of extinct animal species. Similar reports can be traced in northern South America and along the Pacific coasts, downwards from Colombia to Chile.

[16] The Otomí, a nation with its own language had arrived in Central Mexico long before the Nahua tribes. Conquered by the invaders they continued to live and work as a pariah caste in the kingdoms of the Toltecs, Aztecs and the Republic of Tlaxcala. They retained their identity. See Sahagún, Bk. X, Ch. 24.

[17] For more detailed information on Aztec ideas of the afterlife see, Sahagún, Appendix to Bk. III, Chs. 1-3.

[18] The author is wrong. The incidence of irregular sexual behaviour among animals is discussed by D. J. West, *Homosexuality* (Harmondsworth, 1968), pp. 30 ff.

[19] Sahagún, Bk. VIII, Ch. 14. Torquemada, Vol. II, Bk. 12. Ixtlilxóchitl, *Historia*, Ch. 68. Clavijero's comments are still valuable: Bk. VII, Chs. 17-19. For a modern summary see Vaillant, pp. 124-7.

[20] The pre-Conquest cultures of Mesoamerica knew neither grapewine nor alcoholic short drinks. The common mild intoxicant was pulque, made of the self-fermenting juice of the maguey (*agave americana*) and related plants. The name is derived from the Náhuatl *pulioqui* or "decomposed". In pre-hispanic times the name for all species of maguey was *metl* and the name of the product *Iztac octli* (white wine). It had medical applications. Aztec law severely

punished drunkenness, and the explosion of alcoholism after the Conquest was due to the removal of the earlier restrictions.

[21] The problem of alcoholism and its effect on the natives has been widely discussed by the chroniclers. All clerics praise the pre-Spanish restrictions and dwell, sometimes in lurid colours, upon the evils caused by the unlicensed availability of both pulque and Spanish wine. The fullest exposition of the problem and all its aspects is in Agustín de Vetancurt's *Teatro Mexicano*, Pt. I, nos. 107-10, and Pt. II, "Manifesto", in Tratado III.

[22] Anticipating the modern theory of the arrival of the future Amerindians from outside the New World, see José de Acosta, *Historia natural y moral de las Indias* (1590), Bk. I, Ch. 20. The traditional view is expressed by Motolinia, Proem, paras. 31-3; Torquemada, Vol. I, Bk. 1, Chs. 11 ff. and Vol. II, Bk. 6, Ch. 7.

[23] Tlacaélel, an almost legendary Aztec statesman and general, a scion of the royal house and a power behind the throne of kings. I compare him with men like Richelieu of France or Bismarck of Prussia. The chronicles mention him as early as in the reign of Itzcóatl (1426-40) and as late as *c.*1500, which raises the strong possibility of there having been active not one but two princes, bearing the same name and at different times.

[24] The best original eyewitness sources are Hernán Cortés, *Cartas de Relación*, Carta II, and Bernal Díaz del Castillo, *Historia*, Vol. I, Ch. 91.

[25] Copal is the name of several tropical trees which, when incised, yield resin. The genera *Hymenoea* and *Trachylobium* are the most important. Curbaril is one of those trees, the *Hymenaea courbaril*, also known as *anime*.

[26] cf. Sahagún, Bk. III, Appx., Chs. 1-3, for more details.

[27] cf. also: Muñoz Camargo, *Historia de Tlaxcala*, Bk. I, Ch. 18; Ixtlilxóchitl, *Historia*, Ch. 75; Francisco Hernández, *Antigüedades*, Bk. I, Ch. 16; Torquemada, Vol. II, Bk. 13, Ch. 45; Durán, *Historia*, Vol. II, Ch. 51.

[28] The title "New Spain" was introduced by Cortés himself in one of his letters. During the first two hundred years of colonial rule the word "Mexico" was less frequently used, for it actually denoted then only the central core of a vast territory, more or less "Anáhuac" or the heartland of the México-Aztec nation. The use of the word "Mexico" is also confusing for it also denotes the capital city. "New Spain" comprised not only the central core but, more or less, the present states of the modern States of Mexico and Texas, New Mexico, Colorado, Utah, and California, as well as Guatemala, Nicaragua and Honduras.

[29] St Hyppolytus of Rome (*c.*AD 235), a theologian, was martyred in Sardinia. Cassianus of Imola (date unknown), according to legend, refused to sacrifice to the gods and was handed to his pagan pupils, who killed him.

[30] This is erroneous. The author also contradicts himself, for he later gives Cortés's date of birth as 1485. Martin Luther was born on 10 November 1483. He nailed his famous 95 theses to the church-door in Wittenberg in 1517, and not in 1519 as Mendieta states.

[31] The matter of principle in which Cortés was compelled to compromise can be summarized by the question "Who is going to do the work in the new colonial society?" The conquerors, desirous of becoming a landed *hidalguía*, were allotted land and needed hands to work it. The public services also needed labour. The answer, applied in Española, was the *repartimiento*: groups of Indians, usually an entire village, were "entrusted" under the title of *encomienda* to a Spanish landowner, who was henceforth to be responsible for their physical and spiritual welfare. In reality and in most instances the Indians became virtual serfs, some even slaves. The Spanish crown gradually managed to alleviate the worst excesses of the system, while the mendicant orders never failed to inveigh against it. See Las Casas, *Historia de las Indias*, II, pp. 86-90; 374-5; III, 199, 288 and 303. For modern comments see J. H. Parry, pp. 100-5, 165-7, 179-81, 184-6. Also C. H. Haring, *The Spanish empire in America*, Ch. II.

[32] This bull represents the first step in the rise of the Franciscan Order to prominence in the conversion of the natives of America. It conferred upon ordinary friars the immense spiritual powers of the priesthood.

[33] In Chapter 7, Mendieta deals with Paul III's bull, dated 15/11/1535.

[34] Bernal Díaz, Vol. II, Ch. 171; Muñoz Camargo, Bk. III, Ch. 8; Torquemada, Vol. III, Bk. 15, Chs. 10 ff. The arrival of the twelve friars marks an important moment in the consolidation of the conquest, as the domination of the Indians was achieved not only by force but also by their successful conversion to the Christian faith.

[35] Alonso de Molina is the author of the famous first comprehensive dictionary, the *Vocabulario en lengua castellana y mexicana y en lengua mexicana y castellana* (1555-71), which I still consult on occasion. He also wrote a long list of tracts in Náhuatl (*c.*1513-79).

[36] Ome Tochtli, verbally translated means "Two Rabbits". Sahagún mentions him in II, Appx. 3, as a servant of the god of pulque. Diego Durán devotes several paragraphs to him in Vol. I, Ch. 22, paras. 18-23 and 31.

[37] This idyllic picture is also painted by later mendicants, like Torquemada, Remesal and Vetancurt. But it is disputed by the Dominican Thomas Gage, who repeatedly censures the excessive wealth of the monastic institutions he visits. Admittedly he arrived forty years after the completion of Mendieta's work, and he is biased. Let us take a characteristic passage or two: "Vera Cruz: Friar Calvo presented his Dominicans to the prior of the Monastery of St Dominic, who entertained us lovingly with some sweetmeats and everyone with a cup of the Indian drink they called chocolate . . . This refreshment ended, we proceeded to a better one which was a most stately dinner both of flesh and fish. No fowls were spared, many capons, turkey cocks and hens were prodigally lavished to show us the abundance and plenty of provision of that country . . ." (pp. 33-4)

"Jalapa: Here and wheresoever we travelled we still found in the priests and the friars looseness of life and their ways and proceedings contrary to the rules of their profession, sworn by a holy vow and covenant." (p. 43) "It was to us a strange and scandalous sight to see in Jalapa a friar of the cloister riding with his lackey boy by his side on a goodly gelding, with stocking upon his leg and a neat Cordovan shoe upon his foot, with a fine Holland pair of drawers with a lace three inches broad at knee . . . In their talk they would discuss no mortification but mere vanity and worldlines." (p. 44)

[38] Sahagún, Bk. I, Ch. 12, Bk. VI, Ch. 7; Francisco Hernández, Bk. I, Ch. 17; Durán, Vol. I, Chs. 16, 17 & 19; Acosta, Bk. V, Ch. 25; Torquemada, II, Bk. 12, Ch. 11.

[39] Mendieta's chapter refers to a grave conflict with the first Audiencia of New Spain, a clash which lasted from the end of 1528, when Zumárraga arrived, till about 1534. Some of Zumárraga's letters are to be found in *Documentos inéditos*. See also Torquemada, Vol. I, Bk. 5, Ch. 7.

[40] At the time of the conquest and ever since, the Franciscan habit was brown in colour. It consists of a plain woollen tunic with long loose sleeves, and the tunic is held round the waist by a knotted cord. A cape hangs over the shoulder and has a hood affixed to it. The friar usually went barefoot or wore sandals.

[41] Bartolomé de Las Casas (1474-1566), the "Apostle of the Indians", born in Seville, went to Española in 1502, was ordained priest in 1512. Coming to the conclusion that conquistadorial and colonial policy inevitably lead, at best to enslavement, at worst to annihilation of the natives, he joined the Order of St Dominic in 1523. After a relatively brief spell as Bishop of Chiapas (1544-7) he returned to Spain. He was continuously engaged in a fight on many fronts for the human rights of the Indians and had the ear of the rulers of Spain and the Council of the Indies. Among his main works are *Historia de las Indias* and *Brevísima Relación de la destrucción de las Indias*, both consulted herein.

[42] Mendieta refers to the famous Tarascan lacqerware. The lacquer is still produced from a plant louse (*aje*) which is gathered during the rainy season. Other regions producing the ware, at Oaxaca and Guerrero. See Chloe Sayer, *Crafts of Mexico* (London, 1977), Ch. 5.

[43] Sahagún, Bk. IX; Torquemada, Vol. III, Bk. 17, Ch. 1. For more detailed descriptions see P. Kelemen, *Medieval American Art* (2 vols.): on Mexican sculpture see Vol. I, pp. 108-18; on pottery, ibid., pp. 163-74; on metalwork, Vol. II, pp. 272-82; on painting, ibid., pp. 318-32, including codices; and on woodcarving, mosaic, shellwork, and feathercraft, pp. 333-55.

[44] For the life and work of this remarkable man see Book V(1), Ch. 18 and our translation.

[45] The Mexican nations and the Maya did not know the true arch, a curved structure spanning an opening. Instead they either horizontally placed a block of stone, supported at its two ends by vertical pillars. Or alternatively, the Maya, in particular, employed the corbel, which was formed by successive projections of horizontal courses of masonry over an opening until they joined at the apex.

[46] Edwin Williamson, *The Penguin History of Latin America* (London, 1992), p. 192: "In Mexico there were early attempts to train a native clergy, but these were abandoned by the 1560s and thereafter Indians were deemed unfit for the priesthood. Despite some efforts by the authorities in Rome in the early seventeenth century to encourage the recruitment of Indians, the clergy of the Indies remained white until well into the eighteenth century."

[47] The story is taken almost verbatiim from Motolinia's *Historia* (Trat. II, Ch. 6).

[48] The first smallpox epidemic struck in 1520 and undermined Aztec resistance. A second epidemic occurred in 1531.

[49] Fray Juan Baptista, the father-superior and carer of body and soul, was the author of a new translation of the four books of *Contemptus Mundi*.

[50] Mendieta got the viceroy's name wrong. It was Don Gaspar de Zúñiga y Azavedo, Conde de Monterrey (see Vetancurt's *Tratado de la Ciudad de México*), best remembered for sending expeditions to California and for his effort to concentrate nomadic and semi-nomadic Indians in village communities. In English history he is remembered as the commander of La Coruña which he successfully saved from the attentions of Francis Drake. He was Viceroy from 1595 to 1603, and died as Viceroy of Peru in March 1606.

[51] Chichimecs or Chichimeca. In the colonial epoch this word had two meanings: (1) it denoted the barbarians living to the north of the civilized centre; (2) it stood for the early Nahua forefathers who had entered the central lake region after the fall of the Toltec empire. This included nations like the Tepaneca, the Tetzcocoans, the Tlaxcaltecas and, of course, the México-Aztecs.

[52] In his short prologue "al sincero lector", preceding the Spanish edition of 1569, Sahagún refers to the method of Ambrogio Calepino, a native of Bèrgamo. He was one of the earliest Italian lexicographers (*c.*1440-1510). Scion of a noble family, he entered the Order of St Augustine and compiled a dictionary of the Latin language, published in Reggio Emilia in 1502. Sahagún's prologue states that each page of the manuscript is divided into three columns, the first giving his text in Spanish, the second in Náhuatl, and the third in pictograms.

[53] Matlatzincatl, an inhabitant of Matlatzinco, a town and region, identified with the Valley of Toluca and district. Mentioned by Sahagún, Bk. X, Ch. 29, para. 6, Nos. 67 ff.

[54] Mendieta relates the life of this friar in Bk. V(1), Ch. 17. Tecto preceded the twelve Franciscans, arriving in 1523. His Flemish name was Johann Dekkers.

[55] The Franciscan writers following Mendieta all praise Zumárraga. The intrinsic spirituality and sincerity of the man can best be garnered from his extensive correspondence. See *Documentos inéditos*, Nos 5, 8, 12, 16, 23, 25-9.

[56] In a footnote on p. 130 of Trat. III, Ch. 3, Edmondo O'Gorman points out that he has been unable to find this reference in Motolonia's *Historia*, nor in the *Memoriales*.

[57] The story of young Cristóbal of Tlaxcala, who was killed by his pagan father, was told by Motolinia (*Historia*, Trat. III, Ch. 4) and repeated by all Franciscan chroniclers.

[58] The town of Etzatlán has survived. It lies to the west of the city of Guadalajara and on the borders of the State of Nayarit.

[59] Mendieta refers to the major rebellion against the Spaniards which broke out in 1541, the so-called "Mixton War". The rebels repudiated and renounced Christianity, vacated the newly established *reducciones*, took to the hills and canyons and advocated direct recourse to violence. Spanish garrisons were besieged, and even the city of Guadalajara was threatened. Viceroy Don Antonio de Mendoza was forced to organize a proper military campaign and to take the field himself. He defeated the rebels. A good summary can be found in Baltasar de

Obregón, *Historia des los descubrimientos antiguos* (1584; Mexico city, 1988).

60 St Stephen's story is related in Acts (VI and VII). St Sebastian was first pierced with arrows and battered to death with cudgels. Santa Appolonia was struck repeatedly in the face, had her teeth knocked out, and was thereafter burnt. St Thomas of Canterbury (Thomas à Becket) was slain in his cathedral church on 29 December 1170.

61 Torquemada repeats the story. Vetancurt, in his *Menologio Franciscano*, allots the 10th June to him, the very day of his martyrdom.

62 Agustín de Vetancurt gives the date of his death as November 23, 1556.

BIBLIOGRAPHY

(a) Basic text

Mendieta, Gerónimo de, *Historia Eclesiástica Indiana* (*c*.1596): facsimile edn., ed. Joaquín García Icazbalceta, Mexico City, 1980.

(b) Works 1500-1800

Acosta, José de, *Historia natural y moral de las Indias* (1590), ed. E. O'Gorman, Mexico City, 1985.

Clavigero, Francisco Javier, *Historia antigua da México* (1799), ed. Mariano Cuevas, Mexico City, 1976.

Cuevas, Mariano, *Documentos inéditos del siglo XVI para la historia de México* (1914), ed. Genaro García, Mexico City, 1975.

Cortés, Hernando, *Cartas de Relación* (1519-26), ed. Mario Hernández, Madrid, 1985.

Díaz del Castillo, Bernal, *Historia verdadera de la conquista de la Nueva España*, 2 vols. (*c*.1568), ed. Miguel Léon-Portilla, Madrid, 1988.

Duran, Diego, *Historia de las Indias de la Nueva España*, 2 vols. (*c*.1581), ed. Angel María Garibay, Mexico City, 1984.

Gage, Thomas, *Travel in the New World* (1648), ed. Eric S. Thompson, Norman, 1958.

Gómara, Francisco López de, *Historia general del las Indias* (1552), ed. Jorge Gurria Lacroix, Caracas, 1979.

Hernández, Francisco, *Antigüedades de la Nueva España* (1577), ed. Ascensión H. de Léon-Portilla, Madrid, 1986.

Iztlilxóchitl, Fernando de Alva, *Historia de la nación Chichimeca* (*c*.1646), ed. Germán Vázquez Chamorro, Madrid, 1985.

Las Casas, Bartolomé de, *Brevísima Relación de la destrucción de las Indias* (1552), facsimile edn., ed. Manuel Ballesteros, Madrid, 1977.
Historia de las Indias, 3 vols., ed. Agustín Millares Carolo, Mexico City, 1986.

Motolinia, *Toribio de Benavente, Historia de los Indios de la Nueva España* (1541), ed. Edmundo O'Gorman, Mexico City, 1973.

Muñoz Camargo, Diego, *Historia de Tlaxcala* (1576), ed. Germán Vázquez

Chamorro, Madrid, 1986.
Oviedo y Valdés, Gonzalo, *Sumario de la natural historia de las Indias* (1526), ed. Manuel Ballesteros, Madrid, 1986.
Historia general y natural de las Indias, 5 vols. (1535-48), ed. Juan Pérez de Tudela, Madrid, 1992.
Sahagún, Bernardino de, *Historia general de las cosas de Nueva España* (1565-71), ed. Angel María Garibay, Mexico City, 1975.
Torquemada, Juan de, *Monarquía Indiana*, 3 vols. (1615), facsimile edn., ed. Miguel Léon-Portilla, Mexico City, 1986.
Vetancurt, Augustin de, *Teatro Mexicano* and *Monologio Franciscano* (1697), facsimile edn., Mexico City, 1982.

(c) Works written since 1800

Attwater, Donald, *The Penguin Book of Saints*, Harmondsworth, 1965.
Davies, Nigel, *The Aztecs*, London, 1973.
Morison, Samuel Eliot, *Admiral of the Ocean Seas* (1942), London, 1970.
Parry, J. H., *The Spanish Seaborne Empire*, London, 1966.
Prescott, William H., *History of the Conquest of Mexico* (1843), ed. John Foster Kirk, London, 1863.
Thomas, Hugh, *The Conquest of Mexico*, London, 1993.
Vaillant, George C., and Burland, C. A., *The Aztecs of Mexico*, Harmondsworth, 1961.
Wachtel, Nathan, *The Vision of the Vanquished*, Hassocks, 1977.

(d) Pre-Columbian architecture, cities, and culture

Hardoy, Jorge E., *Pre-Columbian Cities*, London, 1973.
Keleman, Pal, *Medieval American Art*, 2 vols., New York, 1969.
Kubler, George, *The Art and Architecture of Ancient America*, Harmondsworth, 1962.
Léon-Portilla, Miguel, *Aztec Thought and Culture*, Norman, 1975.

INDEX

A

abortion 43
Abraham 24
Acapulco 53
Acosta, Father José de 11
Aculma 36
Aculmaitl 36
adultery 43
Aguilar, Gerónimo de (interpreter) 8, 55
Ahuacatlán 88
alcohol, alcoholism 43, 45-7, 68-9, 92-3, 125-6 n.20
Alexander VI, pope 25-6, 27
Almonte, Fray Diego de 69
Alvarado, Pedro de 62
Ambrose, Saint 9
Amonte, Fray Diego de 67
Anáhuac 5, 53-4
Appolonia, Santa 120, 130 n.60
Ascencio, miracle of 75-6
Atacubaya 75
Atlantic ocean 21, 25, 53
Atztlán 11
Augustine, Saint 2
Augustinians, Augustinian order 7
Ayora, Fray Juan de 89, 101
Azores 26

B

Babel
  land of 47
  Tower of 39
Baltasar (founder of Chocoman community) 84
Baptista, Fray Juan 96-7, 100-1, 129 n.49
Barcelona 24

Bassacio, Fray Aranoldo de 99
bawds 44
bell manufacture, native 82
Benavente, Fray Melchior de 107
Benedictines, Benedictine order 27
Benito, religious experience of 86-7
Bernard, Saint 5
Betanzos, Fray Domingo de 110
Bienvenida, Fray Rodrigo de 88, 115
Buil, Father Bernardo 27-9, 123 n.2, 124 n.4

C

Calepino lexicographical system 100, 129 n.52
Calero, Fray Juan, martyrdom of 117-21, 130 n.61
calpixques 48
Cape Verde 26
Caribbean Indians 58
carpentry, native 78, 83, 105
Cartujano, Dionisio 111
Castro, Fray Andrés de 101
Catholic Church 53, 54, 77, 118
Caxacanes (rebels) 118-19
Cebreros, Fray Alonso de 88
Cempoala 56
Charles V, emperor 53, 57, 72, 107, 108
Chichimecs 5, 118, 119, 122, 123, 129 n.51
children, upbringing of 93-4
Chocoman community 84-5
Cholula 38, 39, 84, 86, 96
Chrysostom, Saint 5
Cichicomóztoc, Cave of 36
Cisneros, Fray García de 99
Claire, Saint 115
Clapión, Juan 58-9

STUDIES IN THE HISTORY OF MISSIONS

1. Daniel M. Davies, The Life and Thought of Henry Gerhard Appenzeller (1858-1902): Missionary to Korea
2. Johnathan J. Bonk, The Theory and Practice of Missionary Identification (1860-1920)
3. Samuel J. Rogal, John Wesley's Mission to Scotland 1751-1790
4. James L. Cox, The Impact of Christian Missions on Indigenous Cultures: The "Real People" and the Unreal Gospel
5. Gwinyai H. Muzorewa, An African Theology of Mission
6. J.R. Oldfield, Alexander Crummell (1819-1898) and The Creation of An African-American Church in Liberia
7. Stewart D. Gill, The Reverend William Proudfoot and the United Secession Mission in Canada
8. Harvey J. Sindima, The Legacy of Scottish Missionaries in Malawi
9. Samuel J. Rogal, John Wesley in Ireland, 1747-1789
10. Alan G. Padgett (ed.), The Mission of the Church in Methodist Perspective: The World is My Parish
11. Samuel J. Rogal, John Wesley in Wales, 1739-1790: Lions and Lambs
12. Karl-Wilhelm Westmeier, The Evacuation of Shekomeko and the Early Moravian Missions to Native North Americas
13. Martin E. Lehmann, A Biographical Study of Ingwer Ludwig Nommensen, 1834-1918: Pioneer Missionary to the Bataks of Sumatra
14. Fray Gerónimo de Mendieta, Historia Eclesiástica Indiana: A Franciscan's View of the Conquest of Mexico, critically reviewed, with selected passages translated from the original by Felix Jay